William H. Pivar and Corinne E. Pivar

POWER
REAL ESTATE
E-MAILS &
LETTERS

Fifth Edition

This publication is designed to provide accurate and authoritative information in regard to the subject matter covered. It is sold with the understanding that the publisher is not engaged in rendering legal, accounting, or other professional advice. If legal advice or other expert assistance is required, the services of a competent professional should be sought.

President: Dr. Andrew Temte
Chief Learning Officer: Dr. Tim Smaby
Vice President, Real Estate Education: Asha Alsobrooks
Development Editor: Julia Marti

POWER REAL ESTATE E-MAILS & LETTERS FIFTH EDITION
©2012 Kaplan, Inc.
Published by DF Institute, Inc., d/b/a Dearborn Real Estate Education
332 Front St. S., Suite 501
La Crosse, WI 54601

Printed in the United States of America
Third printing 2013
ISBN: 978-1-4277-1140-3 / 1-4277-1140-2
PPN: 1926-0306

CONTENTS

CHAPTER 3

Solicitations for Expired and For-Sale-by-Owner Listings   51

CHAPTER 4

Responses to Owner Inquiries   67

CHAPTER 5

Residential Buyer Solicitations   81

CHAPTER 6

Land, Business, and Investment Buyer Solicitation   117

CHAPTER 7

Servicing the Listing   137

CHAPTER 8

Buyer E-mails and Letters   195

CHAPTER 9

Breach of Contract and Other Conflict Communications   235

CHAPTER 10

Property Management   253

CHAPTER 11

Broker, Lender, and Attorney Letters   285

CHAPTER 12

Personnel Letters   321

CHAPTER 13

Press Releases   343

CHAPTER 14

Miscellaneous Letters   355

INTRODUCTION

In effective communications, personal contact usually ranks first and telephone conversations, second. This leaves written communications in third place. Written correspondence does, however, have some distinct advantages over other methods of communication. Besides providing a written record, which allows little room to question the message conveyed, the written word can provide clarity of intent often lost in verbal exchanges. Also, at times, writing is the only feasible way to communicate effectively because of the recipient's inaccessibility, the sheer volume of people to be contacted, or the complexity of the information to be shared.

Real estate agents need to use their time effectively, and they must establish and maintain relationships with current and future clients. The fifth edition of *Power Real Estate E-mails & Letters* puts fresh, persuasive, concise letters and e-mails at your fingertips. They will save you valuable time and effort in communication on hundreds of topics, allow you to reach a large number of clients. Individual agents and entire real estate offices can increase their productivity by using these simple templates.

You can easily adapt these templates to your own audience. Many of them include optional or sample information in brackets. When several numbered options are supplied, choose one or use your own words to tailor each letter or e-mail to your specific situation.

These templates are available for download at *www.dearborn.com/recampus/ reeceducators.asp?link=6*. In the PIN-PROTECTED RESOURCES field, enter 773355, and then click "Continue." If you are unable to access the templates after entering the PIN, please e-mail us at *contentinquiries@dearborn.com* for assistance.

By presenting either a letter or e-mail format, we have suggested the method we think is best for a given message; however, this is just our suggestion. You can use these messages in the format that works best for you and your circumstances. Before sending a message to or calling your contacts, make sure you comply with the legislation discussed in the next section.

Legislation You Need to Know

Fax Regulations

The Telephone Consumer Protection Act, as well as FCC regulations, prohibits sending unsolicited advertisements (junk faxes) to a fax machine. The prohibition applies to both businesses and residences. As of July 1, 2005, permission to send fax advertisements can be granted only with a signed written statement that includes the fax number to which the fax may be sent. This requirement effectively rules out the use of fax messages for real estate solicitation purposes.

In the real estate profession, the primary use of the fax is in the transmission of documents, although documents are often transmitted as attachments to e-mails.

It is strongly suggested that signed contracts also be placed in the mail at the time they are faxed or e-mailed.

E-mail Regulations

The CAN-SPAM (Controlling the Assault of Non-Solicited Pornography and Marketing) Act of 2003 established national standards for sending commercial e-mail messages. To protect consumers from being assaulted by misleading unsolicited e-mail messages, unsolicited e-mails must include the following:

- A clear and conspicuous opt-out mechanism that allows the recipient to decline future e-mails from the sender

  Example:

  ☐ Please do not send me any further e-mails about real estate opportunities.

- A functioning return e-mail address

- A valid subject line indicating that the message is an advertisement

- The legitimate physical address of the sender

The CAN-SPAM Act, which is enforced by the Federal Trade Commission (FTC), has made it a misdemeanor to send SPAM with falsified header information. Each violation is subject to a fine of up to $16,000.

National Do Not Call Registry

Under the authority of the Telephone Consumer Protection Act, the FTC and the Federal Communications Commission (FCC) established the National Do Not Call Registry, which applies to interstate and intrastate telemarketing calls. By registering their phone numbers, consumers can be protected from unwanted commercial solicitations. Because the fine for calling someone whose name appears on the National Do Not Call Registry is up to $16,000 per call, it is important that calls made to sell or lease properties or to offer services be made only after checking the registry.

To find out whether a party is on the national registry, a broker can request an account number from the registry's Web site, which can be given to agents. Agents can access the registry at *www.telemarketing.donotcall.gov*. The registry is organized by area code.

A simpler method is to use any of a number of scrubber programs available online. These programs will remove numbers on the national registry from your telemarketing list.

Following are some important general exceptions to the do-not-call rules:

- If you have an existing business relationship with a party (18 months after a purchase or a sale), you can call that party even if that party is listed in the registry.

- After an inquiry, calls may be made to the inquiring party for three months.

- You may call persons who have given you written permission to call.

- You may call commercial telephone numbers. (The registry applies only to residential phones.)

- You may call the numbers on for-sale-by-owner ads or signs. A call may be made as a buyer representative but not as a solicitation for seller representation.

- Calls for purely survey purposes are exempt. However, if any solicitation is included in the call, the call is not exempt from the do-not-call rules.

For detailed information about the registry, check *www.fcc.gov/encyclopedia/do-not-call -list*.

Most states have rules and regulations implementing do-not-call legislation that incur fines for telemarketing violations. The Web site *www.donotcallprotection.com/do_not_call _chart.shtml* will indicate whether these regulations expand on federal requirements.

> **Because of the National Do Not Call Registry, initial buyer and seller solicitations will often be limited to personal contact, letters, or e-mails.**

Personal Contact versus Letters

This book provides some letters for situations in which personal contact is often the desired method, such as presenting offers, requesting price reduction, or dealing with personnel problems. Consider each situation individually; ask yourself what your goal is and what the best method of communication is for that goal. As long as it is feasible, use the best method, whether that includes letters, e-mails, faxes, personal contact, phone calls, or another method. Also, be sure to comply with the regulations described in the previous section.

E-mails versus Letters

As you can readily see from your correspondence, use of the letter as a form of written communication has declined while that of e-mail has increased.

Initial contact correspondence must generally be by letter because you are unlikely to have the e-mail address of the recipient, But once contact has been made, further correspondence will probably be by e-mail.

Advantages of E-mail

Using e-mail rather than letters has several distinct advantages, including the following:

- Speed. Messages are transferred immediately from sender to recipient. The old expression "Strike while the iron is hot!" comes from blacksmiths who shaped iron with a hammer. In order to be effective, the iron had to be red hot. This idea is critically important in sales. When recipients want information, you want them to have it immediately.

- Cost. E-mail is virtually cost-free while mailings can be costly, especially when multiple letters are required such as when canvassing a large area or group.

- Links. E-mail can allow recipients to access your Web site, view property flyers, take a virtual tour of property, obtain your resume, view newsletters, and the like.

- Immediate reply. E-mail allows a recipient to immediately reply to a message, and e-mail strings allow you to view the original e-mail as well as responding e-mails.

Disadvantages of E-mail

Disadvantages of e-mails include the following:

- Unopened e-mails. Recipients are bombarded with numerous e-mails. Because an estimated 80 percent of e-mails sent today are related to sex or pornography, it is understandable that so many e-mails are deleted without being opened. There is a danger that important messages will be deleted if the recipient does not immediately recognize the e-mail as legitimate.

- No second chance. Once an e-mail is dumped, it cannot be readily retrieved if the recipient is having second thoughts.

- Spam blockers. Many small businesses get hundreds of e-mails each week—some legitimate, some not—and it takes a lot of time to sort through and determine which are legitimate. To reduce the number of e-mails reaching their servers, businesses and individuals are using SPAM blockers. Spam is electronic mail regarded as junk mail that is sent to a great many recipients. While many types of blockers are available, they generally are keyed to words and phrases that indicate an unsolicited message. Some apply ratings to words and block e-mails that exceed ratings. Some blockers have a "suspect" file into which they place some messages. Words such as "last chance," "limited opportunity," "new breakthrough," "urgent," "money-back guarantee," and the like will probably be rated. You do not want your e-mails to appear to be SPAM, or they may be blocked.

■ No e-mail address. While difficult for most young people to grasp, a great many individuals do not have an active e-mail address or choose not to use e-mail. For this group, letters are the only means of sending the written word.

When Letters Are Preferred

Personal matters normally should be covered by letter. Examples are condolence cards and letters, personnel matters such as commendations or problems, thank you letters, and even Christmas, birthday, or anniversary cards. You have never seen a batch of Christmas e-mails decorating a fireplace mantle. Handwritten notes show caring, while typed messages tend to be impersonal.

Important communications with attorneys and government officials should usually be written in order to reduce the chance that the message will not receive the attention it deserves.

When you want to contact a particular person but don't have an e-mail address and the party is listed on the National Do Not Call Registry, your only alternatives are a knock on the door or a letter.

Obtaining E-mail Addresses

There are hundreds of suppliers of e-mail lists. Many lists are sorted by zip code. Further selection is possible by family size, age, and even income estimates. Even the use of targeted lists is a shotgun approach to marketing. Most e-mails will never be opened and of those that are, few will be read by parties who have a need you wish to fulfill. Your e-mails will be regarded by most recipients as SPAM.

Lists you compile are far more valuable. Sources for these lists include the following:

■ Your Web site. Create a form that allows viewers to indicate whether they would like to receive data on new listings as soon as they are available based on criteria they provide regarding size, area, price range, and essential features.

■ Open-house registry. Ask attendees whether they would like e-mails about new listings and/or future open houses based on their criteria.

■ People who have responded to ads, signs, or your Web site. Ask whether they want information about new listings.

■ Former buyers and sellers. Ask whether they would like to know what is happening in the area as to listings, sales, or a newsletter.

■ People you meet or talk to. A great many people are curious about listing prices and sales in their area. Simply asking whether they would like to receive e-mail information on new listings and/or sales in their area will result in a great many positive responses.

By supplying information to fulfill needs or just curiosity, your e-mails will have a great likelihood of being read, even if the described property does not fulfill a recipient's needs. It might be a property that the recipient will want to mention to a friend.

Tips for Letters and E-mails

All written messages must accurately convey what the writer intends to say to be effective. To achieve this in your writing, apply the KISS rule—keep it simple and sincere. In other words, your message should follow these guidelines:

- Get to the point quickly.

- Use clear and concise language so readers will not get a message other than what is intended.

- Be honest.

Here are a few additional rules you should follow in professional communication, whether in letters or e-mails:

- The most important attribute of any business communication is clarity. It must convey the writer's message to the reader in an unambiguous manner. One of the keys to achieving clarity is brevity. For this reason, the e-mails in *Power Real Estate E-mails & Letters* are short and to the point. Short, clear messages are more likely to be fully read and understood by the reader.

- Brevity is important. A short message is more likely to be read than a long message. Business communications are likely to be read by people who are as protective of their time as you are of yours. Therefore, the message must be quickly understood. If the reader is not getting the importance of the message within the first 15 seconds, chances are that you need to rewrite your message.

- Ideas expressed in short sentences are easier to grasp than those in long sentences.

- Use separate paragraphs for different points you wish to make.

- Your language level should be about the sixth-grade reading level. You might have an extensive vocabulary, but remember that the purpose of your writing is to communicate, not to impress.

- Use a standard font because some readers have difficulty with italics and cute typefaces.

- Avoid extraneous material that detracts from or obscures the primary message.

Letters

All the letters in this book are laid out in roughly the same format, or a fake letterhead that includes a logo. Your correspondence should be on your company's letterhead and include your company's address.

The logo in each of our letters is followed by blanks that precede the salutation (e.g., Dear Mr. Jones). Those blanks are intended for the date and the recipient's name and address, like this:

[Date]

[Recipient name, title (if applicable)]

[Company name (if applicable)]

[Street address]

[City, state, ZIP]

You will see that some letters in this book contain lists of items identified by a bullet (■) or a check mark (✓). Lists are very effective in sales letters because the reader's eyes are led naturally down the letter.

E-mails

Your e-mail address should include your name or your firm's name. Addresses that do not identify senders are not likely to be opened.

The subject line of your e-mail is very important. The subject should be honest, concise, and clear and should entice the reader to open the e-mail. Examples of such subject lines are as follows:

■ (16 homes) selling for half their former price

■ Your neighbor [Charles White] sold his house in [13] days

■ Home prices [fall] [on the rise] in Hoffman Estates

■ [First] million dollar home sale in Hoffman Estates

■ Foreclosure home bargains in your neighborhood

The e-mails in this book include subject lines that you can use or modify as necessary. If you choose to use a letter as an e-mail, don't forget to include the all-important subject line.

Once the e-mail is opened, the text should reinforce the subject immediately. If the first few sentences don't contain the desired material, there is a good chance the e-mail will be discarded before it is fully read.

As with your other written communications, you should use a standard font in a standard size. Do not use all capital letters because it can make your message look like SPAM.

Marketing Tips

Using Sales E-mails and Letters as Marketing Tools

Sales e-mails and letters are different from most business letters. They are directed ads that are simply requests for business. Real estate sales solicitations are intended to sell either your services or property. In advertising, the acronym *AIDA* is often used. It stands for attention, interest, desire, action. A sales letter should meet these criteria: grab the reader's attention, generate interest, create a desire for the product (or for more information), and result in either action by the recipient or the recipient's anticipation of action by you.

When you wish to target a particular party rather than a group, you can make a solicitation letter more likely to be read by sending it as an overnight letter or using a special service such as FedEx. Because it shows that you regard the message as important, the recipient is less likely to discard it without thought.

The message must grab the reader's attention in the first few sentences. If you have attracted the reader's attention, the entire message, even an extremely long one, will generally be read. Attention-getting headings can be directed to particular interests of the recipient, or they can even be absurd or humorous statements. The heading must, however, quickly lead to a message of interest; if it doesn't, your solicitation letter will be discarded. Keep in mind that people want benefits, and they must be told quickly that benefits are what you are offering them.

In the real estate profession, you should regard the e-mail or letter as a tool to get you through a door. They don't sell property or services—the sale is up to you.

Testing Your Market

Direct mail marketers know that all sales letters are not equally successful. Some letters have phenomenal results, while others fail to generate anything other than mailing expense. Because direct mailing is one of the most costly advertising media in terms of the cost for each contact made, you don't want to waste dollars on mailings that fail to maximize results. Your copy is important, and we have provided you with various copy choices for listing and buyer solicitations. However, copy effectiveness will vary regionally and among target audiences. We therefore suggest that you test your market using different copy so you can concentrate on what works most effectively before you send any mass mailings.

To evaluate effectiveness, you can use different mailing pieces sent to people whose last names begin with different letters. By knowing the number of pieces mailed and the resulting number of appointments, you will be able to track your percentage of success.

Because e-mails have only incidental costs, they are used by many marketers to test different approaches before using mass mailings. While e-mail response percentages will likely be far less than direct mail responses because of the large number of e-mails that are either blocked or discarded unread, the response statistics should indicate which approach will result in the greatest benefit.

Dos and Don'ts of Soliciting by Mail

Following are some dos and don'ts of soliciting listings or buyers by mail.

Dos

1. Your mailing should promise a benefit to the recipient.

2. Personally address all correspondence. Never write "To Occupant." Occupants don't buy or sell real estate—people do.

3. Address each letter to make it look personal to the recipient. Handwritten is best, but not always practical. The letter should also be personalized by using the recipient's name. With computer aid, this is a relatively simple task.

4. Target letters to those likely to be interested in your services. Use mailing lists or reverse directories that will give you the names of residents from their addresses. This rifle approach is better than a shotgun approach, in which much of the shot misses the mark. For example, if your mailing's goal is to locate buyers for low-cost homes with low down payments, consider mailing to families within the service area who live in moderately priced rental units and manufactured homes.

5. Include your card in every letter. If your card has a recent photo of you, its effectiveness increases; your reader now identifies your name with a particular person. Cards should also include your e-mail address and company Web site.

Don'ts

1. Don't use a postage meter, third-class mail, a stick-on address label, or a window envelope. These make the mailing look like junk mail, and junk mail is more likely to be discarded after only a cursory glance.

2. Don't disguise the purpose of the letter by making your mailing appear to be an official government letter or a check. Misleading your readers is unethical, and you want to establish yourself as a professional.

3. Don't use undersized envelopes. Envelopes that are too small force you to make an awkward fold in the letter.

Testimonials

Testimonials are effective and can be included as attachments in mailings and e-mails. If the reader can relate to the person giving the testimonial, by being in similar circumstances or from the same area, the effectiveness of the testimonial increases. To obtain testimonials, all you really have to do is ask. Satisfied buyers and sellers usually respond favorably to such a request. See page 191 to find a sample written request for a testimonial letter.

Color

Color and texture attract attention and can be effectively used in flyers, but e-mails and letters should appear personal. Color makes letters appear to be mass-market pieces and create a negative impression when selling real estate. A light color such as buff or gray can, however, convey a professional image. While slick, hard-coated stock can be used for flyers, letters should be on uncoated stationery. For e-mails, a simple black font can be used for the message, but photos in or attached to the e-mail should be color shots that will print well.

Follow-Up Calls

Follow up your e-mail or letter with a call to your contact. Here are four general tips about making follow-up telephone calls to buyer or seller inquiries, as well as letter recipients (when you are not precluded from making the call by a do-not-call list):

1. Immediately identify yourself and tie your call to your e-mail or letter.

2. Give minimal information. The more information you give over the telephone, the less your chance will be of obtaining a face-to-face meeting.

3. Get information—ask questions. Answering questions with questions is a good technique to use (e.g., if a prospect asks how many vehicles a garage of a certain property fits, ask how many vehicles the prospect has).

4. Make a face-to-face appointment. You should set a time and date to meet the prospective buyers or sellers. You will generally want both parties present when you deal with couples. Use an option of two positive choices, instead of giving prospects the option of not meeting with you: "Would you [and Mrs. Smith] be available at 4:30 this afternoon, or would 5:00 be more convenient?"

Have an Idea for an E-mail or Letter? Contact Us!

The e-mails and letters in this book should satisfy more than 90 percent of an average real estate office's written communication needs. If you think there is a need for letters not included in this book, please let us know so we can add them to later editions. Many of the new e-mails and letters in this edition are the result of reader requests. Contact us at *WilliamPivar620@msn.com.*

Acknowledgments

The following reviewers provided valuable assistance in the creation of this book:

- Doris S. Barrell, GRI, DREI
- Terri Murphy, GRI, CRS, LTG, CREC, Terri Murphy Communications, Inc.
- Margaret Nagel, Chicago Association of REALTORS®, REALTORS® Real Estate School
- Sylvia C. Shelnutt, Sylvia Shelnutt Training and Seminars
- Trish Szego, CRB, CRS, ERA Elite Group, REALTORS®
- William R. "Bill" Zales, MA, ED, Tomlinson Black North Idaho Realty, Inc.

PROMOTING YOURSELF

Letting People Know You Are a Real Estate Agent

We strongly suggest that letters, rather than e-mails, be used for introductory promotion. Enclosed cards should have your photo so recipients can place your face with your name.

Letter to Friend or Acquaintance on Joining Firm

UR
HOME REALTY

_____ ← Date and address

_____
_____
_____

Dear _____:

[1. I am your neighbor at 7318 Elm, the green house on the corner of Elm and Larsen. 2. I am Jeffrey's mother. 3. I enjoyed working with you (on the recent blood drive).]

I have recently joined [UR Home Realty] as a [sales associate]. I am well prepared to meet the real estate needs of all my friends and neighbors.

If you or any of your friends need any real estate services, I would appreciate it if you would think of me.

Sincerely,

_____

Enclosure: ← Card

Note: This letter is written for a new licensee. Besides your personal friends and neighbors, the letter should go to people you do business with, close friends of family members, parents of your children's friends, members of organizations you belong to, and so on. The first paragraph makes certain that the recipient knows who you are. If you have had any positive personal relationship with the addressee, be certain to mention it. Your photo on your card will reinforce this reminder.

Broker Letter to Neighbors of New Salesperson

UR

H O M E   R E A L T Y

_____← Date and address

_____

_____

_____

Dear _____:

[Judith Reilly], [your neighbor] who lives [at 1 1 1 Midvale Lane in Sunshine Estates], has recently joined our firm as [1. a sales associate 2. an associate broker]. [Judith] has been your neighbor for [four] years. [She] and [her husband] have [two children, Lisa, age nine, and Jeffrey, age seven, both of whom attend Midvale School]. [Judith is a graduate of Ohio State and previously worked in marketing.] [She] has just completed our training program and will be specializing in [residential sales] in [Orchard Ridge]. If you or any of your friends have any real estate needs, we hope you will contact [Judith]. I have enclosed one of [her] new cards.

Sincerely,

_____

Enclosure: ← Card

Note: This letter should paint the agent as a person the reader will want to know. It should be mailed over a radius of several blocks around the new employee's home, as well as to the employee's special friends and, if the employee has children, to the parents of the children's friends. The employee's picture should be on the enclosed card so neighbors can identify the employee.

Salesperson Letter to Neighbor

UR
H O M E   R E A L T Y

_____ ← Date and address

_____
_____
_____

Dear _____:

I am your [1. neighbor 2. new neighbor] at [3752 Elm Drive—the white house on the corner in Sunshine Estates].

I am [1. an associate broker 2. a real estate salesperson 3. a REALTOR-Associate®] with [UR Home Realty]. I wanted you to know that I am prepared to [meet any real estate needs that you might have].

If you or any of your friends have any questions concerning real estate, don't hesitate to call me at [602-555-8200].

Sincerely,

_____

Enclosure: ← Card

Note: You might add a handwritten note that says, "I will call you in the next few days to discuss any present or future needs you might have." Don't attach this note if the neighbor is listed on the do-not-call registry. Enclose your card with your photograph. Your card is more likely to be noticed if you attach it to the letter with a paper clip or staple.

Letter to Friend or Acquaintance on Designation or Course Completion

---

UR
HOME REALTY

_____ ← Date and address

_____
_____
_____

Dear _____:

[1. Just a short note to let you know that I have been awarded the professional designation (1. CRS 2. GRI) for use after my name. (1. CRS 2. GRI) stands for (1. Certified Residential Specialist 2. Graduate REALTOR® Institute). To achieve this designation, a REALTOR® must have met the high standards set by the (1. Residential Sales Council 2. National Association of REALTORS®) and have completed a rigorous course of training.]

[2. Just a short note to let you know that I have recently completed the course (Financial Skills for the Residential Specialist). This course, sponsored by the (Residential Sales Council), has prepared me to (better advise buyers and sellers in matters such as mortgage choice, tax implications, and available financial alternatives).]

As a result, I am now better prepared to professionally assist buyers and sellers in meeting their real estate needs. Should you or any of your friends be in need of professional real estate services, I hope you will think of me.

[1. Sincerely, 2. Your friend,]

_____

Enclosure: ← Card

Note: If the letter recipient might not immediately identify you from your name, you should include a first sentence such as the following: [1. I am your neighbor at 7318 Elm, the green house on the corner of Elm and Larsen. 2. I am Jeffrey's Mother. 3. I enjoyed working with you (on the recent blood drive).]

Letter to Friend, Acquaintance, Past Customer, and Client When You Change Offices

---

UR
H O M E   R E A L T Y

_____← Date and address

_____
_____
_____

Dear _____:

Just a note to let you know I am located at a new address. I am now [1. a sales associate 2. an associate broker] with [UR Home Realty] at its office [on Bellflower Boulevard]. I will be able to offer a higher level of service because of management support and the group of dedicated professionals who work together as a team to fulfill both buyer and seller needs.

[1. I will be contacting you in the next few days to find out if any of your friends need my real estate services. I would appreciate any help that you can provide. 2. If you or any of your friends need real estate services, I would appreciate it if you would think of me.]

Sincerely,

_____

Enclosure: ← Card

Note: Enclosing a business card with your photo on it greatly enhances your letter's effectiveness; the reader can then place your face with your name. Mail this letter to friends, neighbors, and acquaintances; service people you do business with; members of organizations you belong to (e.g., social, special interest, or religious groups); friends of family members; the parents of your children's friends; previous buyers and sellers you have dealt with; and your active files of prospective buyers and sellers. The paragraph indicating you will be contacting the recipient should be used only if you are not precluded from calling by the do-not-call rules.

Letter to Friend, Acquaintance, Neighbor, or Former Client Upon Opening Your Own Office

---

UR
HOME REALTY

_____ ← Date and address

_____
_____
_____

Dear _____:

Guess what! I took the big step! No, [1. not marriage 2. I am already married]. I have opened my own office (see the letterhead). I am now an independent broker [1. affiliated with (Century 21) 2. doing business as UR Home Realty].

I am very excited about the move. I offer [1. a full range of investment and residential properties 2. specialized service for homebuyers and sellers in (West Covina)].

If you are in the area, stop by for coffee and a hello! I could also use your help. I would greatly appreciate any referrals you can provide of friends and neighbors who might be considering buying or selling real estate in [West Covina].

Sincerely,

_____

Enclosure: ← Card

Note: Asking for help is an excellent approach to use for a person with whom you are acquainted.

Sold a Home in the Neighborhood

UR

HOME REALTY

_____ ← Date and address

_____
_____
_____

Dear _____:

Just a note to let you know I sold [Tom and Mary Riley's] house at [2731 Briar Place]. They are moving to [Phoenix, Arizona]. I know you will be sorry to lose them as neighbors.

I will let you know about our new neighbors when they move in.

If you or any of your friends and neighbors need real estate advice or services, I hope you will consider me.

[1. Sincerely, 2. Your friend,]

_____

Enclosure: ← Card

Welcome Your New Neighbor

UR
H O M E   R E A L T Y

_____← Date and address

_____
_____
_____

Dear _____:

As I wrote you, I sold [Tom and Mary Riley's] house at [2731 Briar Place].

The buyers are [Ralph and Audrey Sharkey]. They have [a son Ralph, Jr., who is eight years old, a son Thomas who is six, and a daughter Lori who is three].

I hope you welcome them to the neighborhood.

If you or any of your friends need real estate services, I hope you will consider me.

[1. Sincerely,   2. Your friend,]

_____

Enclosure: ← Card

Note: This letter and the prior letter show success. When sellers look for an agent, they want one who succeeds. Always obtain the buyer's permission to give out family information.

Offer to Speak

UR
HOME REALTY

_____ ← Date and address

_____
_____
_____

Dear _____:

I understand that, like all service organizations, you constantly need speakers. Well, I would like to offer my services.

I have prepared a [30-minute] presentation on [1. the dynamic changes in the West-wood real estate market 2. proposed zoning changes and what they mean to you 3. the realistic future of the real estate market. 4. why real estate investment makes sense in today's economy 5. the real estate recovery] that I think will interest most of your members.

I will be calling you in a few days to discuss my proposal.

Yours truly,

_____

Enclosure: ← Card

Note: Your chamber of commerce should be able to give you a list of local service organizations and people to contact. By stating you will be calling, the recipient is forced to consider your offer.

CHAPTER

LISTING SOLICITATIONS

Mass e-mails for listing solicitations generally have not been effective because they are regarded by many people as SPAM and tend to create more of a negative than a positive image of you and your firm. Therefore, letters and postcards are of primary importance.

Warning: It is a violation of federal law to induce people to leave a neighborhood because of fear that values or the quality of life will decline because of changes in race, sex, ancestry, religion, handicap, or familial status in the neighborhood due to new residents moving in.

For specialized mailings, consider using mailing lists. Look under "Mailing Lists" in the Yellow Pages to find lists available in your business area.

If you are mailing a listing solicitation letter to people who may have already listed their home, we recommend adding the following statement to the end of the letters: "If you have already listed your home for sale with another broker, please disregard this letter."

Warning: If a letter is to be followed with a phone solicitation, be aware of federal regulations regarding unsolicited phone calls. Check the do-not-call registry section in the introduction.

Selling Interest—I Have a Buyer

UR
HOME REALTY

_____← Date and address

_____
_____
_____

Dear _____:

I am representing [1. a buyer   2. foreign buyers] who [desire(s)] to purchase [a large income property] such as your property at [1131 Lakeview Terrace].

If you are interested in having your property presented to my [buyer(s)], please contact me directly or through your agent with details and sale price.

Yours truly,

_____

Note: This letter should be sent out with your buyers' knowledge. Never indicate a nonexistent buyer.

Foreclosure Action Has Begun

UR
H O M E   R E A L T Y

_____ ← Date and address

_____

_____

_____

Dear _____:

I may be able to help you to avoid foreclosure.

- I can recommend nonprofit agencies that may be able to help you to restructure your home loan.

- I can work with your lender for a possible short sale that will forgive mortgage debt should your mortgage exceed your equity.

- I can evaluate your property and estimate what you might realize from an immediate sale, as well as show you how such a sale can be accomplished.

If you would like to explore any of these possibilities, please contact me for a no-cost, no-obligation consultation.

Yours truly,

_____

Note: Public notice of commencement of foreclosure actions are published in legal newspapers.

We Move Houses

UR
H O M E   R E A L T Y

_____ ← Date and address

_____
_____
_____

Dear _____:

Did you know that

We Move Houses? (No Size Limit)

We can find a new owner for your home and, if you wish, have you in a new home in record time.

Want to know how we do it? With a lot of hard work! We develop a marketing plan for a property and then work the plan.

Call me if you wish to know how we would customize a marketing plan for your home. We also offer an electronic comparative market analysis that indicates what you will likely receive from the sale of your home in today's marketplace. This service is provided without cost or obligation on your part.

If you would like to receive e-mail notification of new listings and sales in your area, please contact me by phone or e-mail [agent@urhome.com].

Sincerely,

_____

P.S. If you have already listed your home for sale with another broker, please disregard this letter.

Enclosure: ← Card

Note: You can enclose the No-Cost Market Analysis Certificate on page 65 with this letter.

Want to Know the Value?

UR
H O M E   R E A L T Y

_____ ← Date and address

_____
_____
_____

Dear _____:

Did you know that

Rumpelstiltskin

was able to turn straw into gold? We have achieved the same performance with real estate.

Let me show you what a sale of your property at [622 North Elm] could mean in terms of actual cash in your hands.

Call or e-mail me for a prompt market analysis, at no cost or obligation, to determine the amount of cash a sale of your property should yield.

Yours truly,

_____

P.S. If you would like to receive e-mail notification of real estate [1. activity 2. sales and listings] in [Crawford Heights], please contact me by phone or e-mail [agent@ urhome.com].

If you have already listed your home for sale with another broker, please disregard this letter.

Enclosure: ← Card, No-Cost Market Analysis Certificate (see page 65)

Note: This type of letter can be used for cold canvassing, but it would be especially strong if mailed to people who have financial difficulties because of liens, bankruptcy proceedings, foreclosure, divorce, death in the family, criminal action, or automobile repossession. Much of this information is available at your county courthouse or legal newspapers.

Why Sell in This Market?

UR

H O M E   R E A L T Y

_____ ⟵ Date and address

_____
_____
_____

Dear _____:

Why Sell Your Home in This Market?

1. Values are down.

2. There is economic uncertainty.

These are actually reasons why, in today's market, you will be able to buy a new home better suited to your needs in the area you want at a price that would have been impossible just a short time ago. In addition, low interest rates will further reduce the true cost of a new home.

If you would like to explore this possibility, I can supply you with a supported estimate of the present value of your home, as well as show you homes that the proceeds from the sale of your home will enable you to buy. This information will be provided to you at no cost or obligation. Want more information? Call or e-mail me today.

Yours truly,

_____

P.S. If you would like to receive e-mail notification of listings and sales in your area, please contact me by phone or e-mail [agent@urhome.com].

Enclosure: ⟵ Card

Only [Seven] Days to Sell

UR

H O M E   R E A L T Y

_____← Date and address

_____
_____
_____

Dear _____:

It took

Only [Seven] Days to Sell!

That's right, it took just [seven] days for [UR Home Realty] to sell the home of the [Clarence Jones family] at [2738 West Wilson]. We hope you will welcome your new neighbors, [Henry and Jean Watson]. [They have two children: Lisa, nine, and Henry, Jr., six.]

In the [seven] days it took to sell the [Joneses'] house, we actually had several other prospective buyers who would like to live in your neighborhood.

If you would like, we can do a comparative market analysis that shows what your home might bring in today's market. We will supply this service without any cost or obligation in the hope that when you consider selling, you'll think of [UR Home Realty]. If you want to take advantage of our offer, call me today.

Yours truly,

_____

P.S. If you would like to be kept up to date on listings and sales in your neighborhood by e-mail, please call or e-mail me to be put on our e-mail list. [agent@urhome.com]

If you have already listed your home for sale with another broker, please disregard this letter.

Enclosure: ← Card

Note: This mailing should be restricted to the area of a recent neighborhood sale. By providing information that is likely to be of interest and by asking the recipient to welcome a new neighbor, you increase the likelihood of the entire letter being read. Do not include personal information about buyers or sellers without their permission. You could enclose the No-Cost Market Analysis Certificate on page 65 with this letter.

Home Sold—Neighborhood Solicitation

UR

H O M E   R E A L T Y

_____ ← Date and address

_____
_____
_____

Dear _____:

We have just sold the home of your neighbor [Mary Atkins] at [1713 Euclid Avenue]. The new buyers are [Henry and Jean Watson]. [They have three children: Lisa, eight, Henry, Jr., six, and Mary, four.] I hope you will welcome them to the neighborhood.

In advertising the [Atkinses'] home, we received a number of inquiries from other families who consider your neighborhood a desirable place to live. We would like to help them, but we need homes to sell.

If you or any of your neighbors are considering a move, I would appreciate hearing from you.

Yours truly,

_____

P.S. If you would like to receive e-mails concerning new listings and sales in [Westwood], please contact me by phone or e-mail. [agent@urhome.com]

If you have already listed your home for sale with another broker, please disregard this letter.

Enclosure: ← Card

Note: Never give out information about a buyer without the buyer's permission.

Farewell to Your Old Neighbors—Welcome to the New Ones!

UR

HOME REALTY

_____← Date and address

_____
_____
_____

Dear _____:

Farewell to Your Old Neighbors—Welcome to the New Ones!

It must seem that you have said goodbye to many old neighbors; [UR Home Realty] has sold [19] homes in [Truesdale Estates] in the last [six] months. On the bright side, you have the opportunity to make many new friends.

There are good reasons for our phenomenal success in [Truesdale Estates], and I would like the opportunity to discuss them with you.

I would also like to prepare a comparative market analysis that indicates the likely sales price of your home in today's marketplace, should you decide to sell. We perform this service without any cost or obligation on your part! If this interests you, please give me a call.

If you would like to receive e-mails concerning the new listings and sales in [Truesdale Estates], let me know by phone or e-mail. [agent@urhome.com]

Hoping to be of service,

_____

If you have already listed your home for sale with another broker, please disregard this letter.

Enclosure: ← Card

A Neighbor Listed with Us

UR
H O M E   R E A L T Y

_____ ← Date and address

_____
_____
_____

Dear _____:

Do You Want to Know What Your Neighbors Did?

Your neighbors [John and Mary Smith] at [1 1 1 Midvale Lane] have just placed their home for sale through [UR Home Realty].

They will be able to take advantage of [1. the exceptional demand our office has been experiencing in your area. 2. the recent upturn in the real estate market].

If you want to know what a sale of your home can mean for you in dollars and common sense, I can provide you with a market analysis showing you what to expect from a sale of your home. This service is provided at no cost or obligation.

[1. I will call you in the next few days to learn whether you want to take advantage of this offer and also to ask for your help in choosing a new neighbor. 2. If you want to take advantage of this offer, or if you know someone who might like to be your neighbor, please call me.]

Yours truly,

_____

P.S. If you would like to be on our e-mail list to receive notification of new listings and sales in your neighborhood, please visit our Web site at [agent@urhome.com]

If you have already listed your home for sale with another broker, please disregard this letter.

Enclosure: ← Card

Note: You could include the No-Cost Market Analysis Certificate on page 65 with this letter. Besides soliciting listings, this letter lets neighbors know that property is available, and it can serve to locate buyers. Indicate that you will call only if the neighbor is not listed on the do-not-call registry.

Help Us Find a Home for a Future Neighbor #1

UR
HOME REALTY

_____ ← Date and address

_____
_____
_____

Dear _____:

Can You Help a Future Neighbor?

We need a [three]-bedroom home in your neighborhood for a [young family]. [The husband is an engineer and the wife is a schoolteacher. They have an 11-year-old son and a daughter who is 7. They would like to relocate before school starts in September and desire a home within walking distance of Midvale School.]

[1. I will be calling you in a few days to determine whether 2. Please call me if] you know of anyone in the neighborhood who might consider selling their home to this fine family.

Sincerely,

_____

Enclosure: ← Card

Note: The heading should get this letter read. The prospective buyers should be real people with whom you are working, and they should be presented in a positive manner. People will go out of their way to help specific people, but not necessarily people in general.

Not only is this an effective listing canvassing tool, but also the effort expended for the buyers you are working for will serve to make them feel indebted to you, reducing the chances of their contacting other agents. Obtain the prospective buyer's permission before sending out this letter.

Indicate that you will be calling only if the addressee is not on the do-not-call registry.

Help Us Find a Home for a Future Neighbor #2

UR
HOME   REALTY

_____ ← Date and address

_____
_____
_____

Dear _____:

We are seeking a [three-bedroom, two-bath] home [1. close to 2. within walking distance of 3. within golf-cart distance of] [1. the Midvale Elementary School 2. the Palm Dale Country Club 3. Horton Corporation]. The home is needed for [a young family who has a nine-year-old son and a seven-year-old daughter.] [They are transferring to the area and would like to become members of your country club.]

[1. I will be calling you in the next few days to ask for 2. Please call me if there are] any suggestions you can provide in helping us find a home for this fine family.

Yours truly,

_____

Enclosure: ← Card

Note: Describe the buyers you are working with in a positive fashion. People like to help nice people, especially when they have common interests. This solicitation is extremely effective when mailed to the members of a particular group, such as golf clubs, health clubs, specific companies, and so on. By using your buyer's interests, you can target people in the desired area who have similar interests. Because this solicitation is so effective, you should consider asking prospective buyers whether they prefer to live within walking distance of any school, club, or the like. By contacting the group, you should be able to obtain a membership list. A letter such as this also serves to obligate the buyers. Obtain the buyers' permission to send this letter. You may indicate you will call the owners only if they are not on the do-not-call registry.

We're Sold Out!

UR
HOME REALTY

_____ ← Date and address

_____
_____
_____

Dear _____:

I'm sorry but

We're Sold Out!

We don't have a home to sell in [Chase Subdivision]. Our inventory is sold out!

If you are at all contemplating selling your home, consider acting now to take advantage of this unusual situation. Call or e-mail me today. I can prepare an electronic comparative market analysis without any cost or obligation whatsoever, a service of [UR Home Realty]. This analysis will tell us how much cash a sale can be expected to yield.

Yours truly,

_____

P.S. If you would like to be on our e-mail list to receive new listing and sales information in your neighborhood, please visit our Web site at [www.urhome.com].

If you have already listed your home for sale with another broker, please disregard this letter.

Enclosure: ← Card

Note: You could enclose the No-Cost Market Analysis Certificate on page 65 with this letter. Before you indicate that an unsolicited call will be made, check the do-not-call registry.

I Apologize

UR
HOME REALTY

_____ ← Date and address

_____
_____
_____

Dear _____:

I Apologize

If you want to buy a home in [Claridge Estates], I don't really have much to show you. Demand has been steady, and the few owners who have taken advantage of the market quickly sold their homes. However, if you really want to buy, call me and I will put your name on my list of buyers, and I will call or e-mail you as soon as properties come on the market.

Now, if you are interested in selling, that's a different story! I can prepare a report of recent comparable sales indicating the price range we can anticipate from a sale of your home in the current market. This service is at no cost or obligation to you.

Want to take advantage of our offer? Call or e-mail me today.

Yours truly,

_____

P.S. If you would like to be on our e-mail list to receive new listing and sales information in your neighborhood, please sign up on our site, [www.urhome.com].

If you have already listed your home for sale with another broker, please disregard this letter.

Enclosure: ← Card

Note: You could enclose the No-Cost Market Analysis Certificate on page 65 with this letter.

Area Activity Report

UR

H O M E   R E A L T Y

_____ ← Date and address

_____
_____
_____

Dear _____:

Your Neighborhood's on the Move!

I thought you might be interested in what's happening around you. During [August], there were [seven] sales in [Sunnybrook Acres].

[Home Information]	[Square Feet]	[Price]
1. [3BR, 2 Bath, 8 years old]	[1,950]	[$327,000]
2. _____	_____	_____
3. _____	_____	_____
4. _____	_____	_____
5. _____	_____	_____
6. _____	_____	_____
7. _____	_____	_____

If you want to know what to expect from a sale of your home, call for a no-obligation electronic comparative market analysis.

Sincerely,

_____

P.S. If you would like to be on our e-mail list to receive new listing and sales information in your neighborhood, please visit our Web site at [www.urhome.com].

Enclosure: ← Card

Note: Don't give out sales information by address unless you have authority to do so. Many sales contracts used by agents allow this information to be disclosed. The Area Activity Report is a good monthly report that will be read. You do not have to be the sales or listing agent on the properties listed in the report.

What's Happening in Your Neighborhood?

UR

HOME REALTY

_____ ← Date and address

_____
_____
_____

Dear _____:

Do you know what's happening in your neighborhood?

We Are Zeroing in on Your Home!

The following properties have been recently sold [near your home] [by UR Home
Realty]:

[3BR Stardust Lane]	[$289,500]
[2BR Stardust Circle]	[$267,500]
[3BR Lynn Court]	[$214,500]
[4BR Lynn Court]	[$374,500]

Would you like to see a Sold sign in front of your property as well?

If you would like to be on our e-mail list to receive the latest information on property
listings and sales in the area, please visit our Web site at [www.urhome.com]. If you
would like to receive a free, no-obligation comparative market analysis indicating
what you can expect to receive from a sale of your home, please call me.

Yours truly,

_____

P.S. If you have already listed your home for sale with another broker, please disregard
this letter.

Enclosure: ← Card

Note: Do not give exact addresses of particular homes without permission of both
buyer and seller.

Newsletter Offer—Postcard

WHAT'S HAPPENING IN THE NEIGHBORHOOD?

Receive a free e-newsletter about [Hampton Acres]. Events, new residents, city hall actions, property markets, and more!

Call [Tom Jones] at (602) 555-8200.

Or check our Web site at *www.urhome.com* to be placed on our [monthly] e-mail list (you may unsubscribe at any time).

H O M E   R E A L T Y

Note: This message could also be used as a door hanger or e-mail to residents for whom you have e-mail addresses. The postcard allows complete coverage for farming purposes.

Many offices find that newsletters are effective marketing tools. If you don't want to start from scratch, there are many real estate newsletters advertised on the Internet that allow you to customize with local material.

General Survey Letter

UR
H O M E   R E A L T Y

_____ ← Date and address

_____
_____
_____

Dear _____:

We would appreciate your help in a survey we are conducting of [the Orchard Ridge Subdivision]. Your assistance will help us target our marketing efforts. Please complete the short questionnaire and return it to us in the enclosed postage-paid envelope.

■ How many years have you lived in [Orchard Ridge]? _____

■ How many homes have you owned before your present residence? _____

■ What do you like most about [Orchard Ridge]? _____
_____

■ What do you like least about [Orchard Ridge]? _____
_____

■ Would you recommend your neighborhood to friends seeking to relocate?
_____

■ Why? _____
_____

■ Would you like to receive e-mails concerning sales and new listings in [Orchard Ridge]?   ☐ Yes (Sales)   ☐ Yes (New listings)   ☐ No

Name: _____   E-mail address: _____

Thank you for your help.

_____

Enclosure: ← Card, postage-paid envelope

Note: This low-key survey is likely to give you a chance to contact the recipient by e-mail. After providing listing and sales information (with photos), you could offer a no-cost comparative market analysis.

Buyer/Seller Referral

UR

H O M E   R E A L T Y

_____ ← Date and address

_____
_____
_____

Dear _____:

Our mutual friend [Mary Hopkins] suggested that I contact you. As you may know, I [1. found a new home for Mary 2. successfully helped Mary sell her home].

I will be contacting you in the next few days to discuss [1. your real estate needs 2. the marketing of your home].

Yours truly,

_____

Enclosure: ← Card

Note: Do not make telephone contact if the recipient is on the do-not-call registry. If the recipient is listed on the registry, contact should be personal.
Do-not-call restrictions do not allow exceptions for referrals.

Referral—Thank You

UR
H O M E   R E A L T Y

_____ ← Date and address

_____
_____
_____

Dear _____:

We know we have successfully met buyer and seller needs when we get referrals. I was very happy to receive your referral of [Jacob and Naomi Jones]. I am working with [Mr. and Mrs. Jones] and feel certain I will [1. find them a new home 2. be able to locate a buyer for their home].

Again, many thanks,

_____

Enclosure: ← Card

Sorry I Missed You

UR
H O M E   R E A L T Y

Sorry I Missed You!

I was checking your neighborhood for real estate needs. If you would like to know the present value of your home, I can provide you with a comparative market analysis that indicates what you could expect to sell your home for in our present market. We provide this service at absolutely no cost or obligation.

────── Call Me As Soon As Possible ──────

P. S. If you would like to be on our e-mail list to receive the latest listing and sales information in your neighborhood, visit our Web site at [www.urhome.net].

Clarence Beyer
Sales Associate
UR Home Realty [555-555-8200]
Cell Phone [555-555-6173]

UR
H O M E   R E A L T Y

Clarence Beyer
Sales Associate
UR Home Realty [555-555-8200]
Cell Phone [555-555-6173]
E-mail: [Agent@urhome.com]

Photo

Note: This is a door hanger to leave on the front door when no one answers. If the door hanger is perforated, the business card can be detached.

Birth of Son or Daughter
(Condominium or Manufactured Home Owner)

UR
H O M E   R E A L T Y

_____ ← Date and address

_____
_____
_____

Dear _____:

Congratulations on the birth of your [1. son John 2. daughter Mary Jane]! It won't be long before [1. he 2. she] will be running around in seemingly perpetual motion. You probably will be considering purchasing a home with your own backyard for [1. John 2. Mary Jane].

I can help you to not only find the perfect home but also to sell your [1. condominium 2. manufactured home]. Our office provides an electronic comparative market analysis that indicates what you could expect to receive on a sale of your [1. condominium 2. manufactured home] in today's market. We provide this service without any cost or obligation on your part! We can also analyze your finances and explain current lender requirements and loan opportunities.

[Please call or e-mail me at [agent@urhome.com] I can help you meet your real estate needs.]

Yours truly,

_____

P.S. If you have already listed your home for sale with another broker, please disregard this letter.

Enclosure: ← Card

Note: From the addresses in birth announcements in local newspapers, you can ascertain whether the parents live in condominiums or manufactured homes. These parents are likely prospects for both a listing and a sale. You could enclose the No-Cost Market Analysis Certificate on page 65 with this letter.

Graduation of Son or Daughter

UR
H O M E   R E A L T Y

_____ ← Date and address

_____
_____
_____

Dear _____:

Congratulations! I bet that you feel both proud and glad your [1. son 2. daughter] has graduated from [1. high school 2. college]. Now you will probably be able to think about your own needs.

Perhaps you want a smaller home, or the low-maintenance lifestyle of an apartment, condominium, or manufactured home. Perhaps you want to retire and head for a warmer climate. Whatever your housing needs are, I can help you.

Before you make any decisions, you should know exactly where you stand. I will be happy to furnish you with a comparative market analysis that indicates the present value of your home. In this way, you will know what to expect should you decide to sell. Please call me if you would like this analysis, offered without cost or obligation.

Yours truly,

_____

P.S. If you have already listed your home for sale with another broker, please disregard this letter.

Enclosure: ← Card

Note: This letter is most effective when mailed to single parents. This information may be available from graduation announcements. You could enclose the No-Cost Market Analysis Certificate on page 65 with this letter.

Marriage of Son or Daughter

UR

HOME REALTY

_____ ← Date and address

_____
_____
_____

Dear _____:

Congratulations! Now that your [1. son 2. daughter] is married, you probably feel happiness mixed with sadness and even relief. It is, however, a time when you can begin thinking more about your own needs.

Perhaps you want a smaller home, a low-maintenance home, or a different lifestyle. You might even be considering retirement. Whatever your housing needs are, I can help you.

Before you make any decisions, you should know your complete financial picture. I'll be happy to prepare an electronic comparative market analysis that indicates the present value of your home. In this way, you will know what to expect should you decide to sell.

If you would like this analysis without any cost or obligation whatsoever, call or e-mail me for a prompt response.

Yours truly,

_____

P.S. If you have already listed your home for sale with another broker, please disregard this letter.

Enclosure: ← Card

Note: This letter is especially effective when sent to single parents. You could enclose the No-Cost Market Analysis Certificate on page 65 with this letter.
If there was a photo in the newspaper of the bride and/or groom, cut it out and include it with your letter. Write "Thought you might like an extra copy" on a sticky note you attach to the clipping.

Retirement

UR
HOME REALTY

_____ ← Date and address

_____
_____
_____

Dear _____:

Congratulations on your retirement! I wish you many happy years to enjoy the fruits of your labor.

Many retirees move to areas such as Florida or Arizona for the mild climate, relaxed lifestyle, and the common interests of retirement communities, as well as the lower housing costs. Chances are that you could sell your home, buy a nice home or condominium in Florida or Arizona, and have cash left over to invest in order to supplement your retirement income.

Before you make any decisions, you should first know exactly where you stand. I will be happy to prepare a computer-generated comparative market analysis that indicates the value of your home in the present market. In this way, you will know what to expect if you decide to sell. [1. I will be calling you in the next few days to find out whether   2. Call me if] you would like to obtain this analysis, offered without any obligation on your part.

Yours truly,

_____

P.S. If you have already listed your home for sale with another broker, please disregard this letter.

Enclosure: ← Card

Note: Employee newsletters are an excellent source of retiree information. Some personnel offices also provide this information. You could enclose the No-Cost Market Analysis Certificate on page 65 with this letter.
Always check the do-not-call registry before any unsolicited call is made to sell services.

Builder Solicitation—Building Permit

_____

UR
H O M E   R E A L T Y

_____ ← Date and address

_____
_____
_____

Dear _____:

I was pleased to learn that you have taken out a construction permit for another new home at [3476 Poplar Lane]. New construction has greatly enhanced the desirability of the community and has resulted in increased sales activity in the neighborhood.

I believe the most effective new-home marketing effort really starts before construction begins. A plan and specifications review by a marketing specialist often reveals that some costly features are not essential, while other features can increase the home's salability and sales price far beyond their additional cost. I will be [1. calling 2. contacting] you in a few days to schedule a meeting so we can discuss ways to ensure a quick sale while maximizing your profits.

Yours truly,

_____

Enclosure: ← Card

Note: Send this letter for building permits taken out in the builder's name. Homes being built for a buyer usually have the permit in the buyer's name.

This letter offers benefits to the reader. Mentioning an impending call encourages the reader to consider a review of the plan features.

The do-not-call registry generally does not apply to business phones, but it does apply to residential phones.

Owner Solicitation—Building Permit

UR

H O M E   R E A L T Y

_____ ← Date and address

_____
_____
_____

Dear _____:

I was happy to learn that you have taken out a construction permit for your new home in [Orchard Ridge]. I am certain that you will be happy with your decision because the area offers exceptional residential benefits.

While it will be some time before you are able to enjoy your new home, it is not too early to consider a marketing plan for your present home at [1812 Thomas Drive].

I would be happy to meet with you to develop a marketing plan for your home that will best meet your needs. There is absolutely no obligation on your part, and I hope that when you see what we can do, you will consider having [UR Home Realty] as your representative.

You may learn more about our services by visiting our Web site at [www.urhome.com].

A call or e-mail can start the marketing process.

Yours truly,

_____

P.S. If you have already listed your home for sale with another agent, please disregard this letter.

Enclosure: ← Card

Note: When a building permit is taken out in an individual's name and a directory search indicates that the party is living in other than an apartment, you can expect that the home will be placed on the market.

Listing Solicitation—Out-of-Town Owner

UR
HOME REALTY

_____ ← Date and address

_____
_____
_____

Dear _____:

As you undoubtedly know, owning property that is located far away from you can be challenging. Problems tend to become magnified by distance and often lead to anxiety and frustration.

[1. Right now, we are experiencing an exceptional market. 2. Despite current market conditions, we are selling property.] I believe that we can sell your [three-bedroom home] in [Midvale Heights] at an attractive price. In fact, we would be happy to prepare, without obligation to you, a comparative market analysis to show you what you might expect to receive from a sale in the present market.

[1. I will be calling you in the next few days to ascertain your interests in selling your property. 2. Call me at [800-555-1111] if you would like more information about what we can do for you.]

Yours truly,

_____

P.S. If you have already listed your home for sale with another agent, please disregard this letter.

Enclosure: ← Card

Note: The knowledge of an imminent call makes an owner consider the option of selling. Indicate a call only if the owner is not on the do-not-call registry. This letter has greater effect if the property has vacancies, needs repair, or has had recent evictions. A good source of leads is problems found in public records. You could enclose the No-Cost Market Analysis Certificate on page 65 with this letter. Having an 800 number increases the likelihood of a call from outside the local telephone area.

Owners Who Have Homes for Rent

UR
H O M E   R E A L T Y

_____ ← Date and address

_____
_____
_____

Dear _____:

Do You Really Want to Rent Your Property?

Consider these points:

- Do you understand that rental income from a single-family home seldom makes economic sense when compared with the likely sale price?

- Do you understand that when you rent your home, you place a tenant in charge of a valuable asset? Consider the dangers of a careless tenant.

- Do you understand that should you decide to sell after you rent the property, your chance of a sale could be diminished because of the tenant's rights?

- Do you understand how lengthy and costly it can be to evict a problem tenant who falsely makes claims such as discrimination, retaliatory eviction, that the property was not in habitable condition, or even an ownership interest?

- Do you understand how desirable your home would be considered by many potential buyers?

- Do you understand that even with the current market conditions, you might realize an amount far greater than you imagined?

Let us show you how we can sell your home now and what you could expect to receive from a sale. We can furnish market analysis without any cost or obligation on your part.

[1. I will be contacting you in the next few days to discuss the advantages that a sale offers you over renting. 2. Please call me if you would like to know what a sale can do for you.]

Yours truly,

_____

Enclosure: ← Card

Note: The paragraph indicating you will be contacting the recipient should be used only if the party is not on the do-not-call registry. However, if the contact will be personal, and not by phone, you can indicate you will make contact even if the party is on the do-not-call registry.

Listing Solicitation—Apartments

UR
H O M E   R E A L T Y

_____ ← Date and address

_____
_____
_____

Dear _____:

[1. **Tenant Problems?** 2. **Headache Renters?**]

Have you considered the advantage of having your apartment equity in management-free corporate bonds, tax-free municipals, or . . . ?

■ No rents to try to collect!

■ No vacancies to worry about!

■ No repairs to make!

■ No tenant complaints!

■ No building inspector problems!

■ No evictions!

I will be [1. calling you   2. contacting you] in a few days to determine your interest in selling.

Incidentally, we can perform an electronic comparative market analysis—at no cost or obligation to you—that indicates what you can expect to receive from the sale of your apartment building.

Yours truly,

_____

If you have already listed your property for sale with another broker, please disregard this letter.

Enclosure: ← Card

Note: Besides general mailings to owners of apartments, consider checking public records for problem property plagued by evictions, unpaid taxes, code violations, and so on. You could enclose the No-Cost Market Analysis Certificate on page 65 with this letter.

If you will place the call to the owner's residence, make sure the owner is not listed on the do-not-call registry.

Listing Solicitation—Lot or Land #1

UR
HOME REALTY

_____ ← Date and address

_____
_____
_____

Dear _____:

Is Your Dirt Gathering Dust?

Your [1. lot   2. 20 acres] located on [Dillon Road] is costing you money:

- ▉ Taxes
- ▉ Opportunity costs in earnings that would be received from investing the sale proceeds

Want to Know What Your Dirt Is Worth?

Contact me and I will show you what you could expect to receive in today's [1. advantageous   2. booming   3. recovering] market.

Yours truly,

_____

Enclosure: ← Card

Listing Solicitation—Lot or Land #2

UR
HOME REALTY

_____ ← Date and address

_____
_____
_____

Dear _____:

When Is the Best Time to Sell [1. a Vacant Lot 2. Land]?

The answer is easy: when there are buyers! Right now we are dealing with buyers who have expressed interest in [1. a lot 2. acreage] such as your [1. lot on Dillon Road 2. 20 acres in Bloomington Township].

If you would like to know what your [1. lot 2. land] should sell for in the current market, please contact me.

Yours truly,

_____

Enclosure: ← Card

Note: Never indicate a nonexistent buyer interest.

Listing Solicitation—Lot or Land #3

UR
H O M E   R E A L T Y

_____ ← Date and address

_____
_____
_____

Dear _____:

I may have a buyer for your [1. lot   2. land] on [Dollar Road]. If you are interested in exploring the possibility of a sale, contact me at once at 602-555-8200 or e-mail me at [agent@urhome.com].

Yours truly,

_____

Enclosure: ← Card

Note: Only use this type of letter, which indicates a possible buyer, when you are actually working with a prospective buyer for similar property. This letter should give you an exceptional response rate. Because many owners of lots and land are owners of multiple properties, the contacts made could be valuable for both listings and sales.

SOLICITATIONS FOR EXPIRED AND FOR-SALE-BY-OWNER LISTINGS

We recommend that you use letters in these situations. Even if you have proper e-mail addresses, unsolicited e-mails will likely be considered SPAM.

Expired Listing #1

UR
H O M E   R E A L T Y

_____ ← Date and address

_____
_____
_____

Dear _____:

I [1. showed your home while it was listed with (Kenco Realty) 2. toured your home when it was first listed with (Kenco Realty)].

I have some suggestions that I believe will help sell your home. If you contact me, I will be happy to go over my ideas for a successful sale.

Yours truly,

_____

P.S. If you have again listed your home with another agent, please disregard this letter.

Enclosure: ← Card

Note: Ideas for selling might include a better way to prepare the house to show, a redirection of advertising, a price adjustment, and so forth.

Expired Listing #2

UR
HOME REALTY

_____ ← Date and address

_____
_____
_____

Dear _____ :

[I was surprised that your home failed to sell while it was listed for sale.]

Did you know that the three most common reasons a home fails to sell are these:

- ■ Failure to target the marketing toward the most likely buyer
- ■ Improper pricing
- ■ A negative first impression (which in many cases could be corrected with minimum expenditure)

I would like to offer my experience at no cost or obligation to you. I will analyze your home and give you my recommendations in writing as to how your home can be sold.

[1. If you are interested in a no-cost or obligation analysis as to why your home failed to sell, please contact me. 2. I will stop by to see whether you are interested in a no-cost or obligation analysis of why your home failed to sell.]

Yours truly,

_____

P.S. If you have already listed your home for sale with another broker, please disregard this letter.

Enclosure: ← Card

Note: When you meet with the owners, go over all prior agents' communications with the owners to ascertain how the agents' activities were directed.

For-Sale-by-Owner Listing #1

UR
HOME REALTY

_____ ← Date and address

_____
_____
_____

Dear _____:

Can You Pass the Owner's Quiz?

■ Do you have a buyer?

■ Have you qualified the buyer on financial ability?

■ Is your buyer contractually obligated to the purchase?

■ Has your buyer been able to arrange the necessary financing?

If all the answers are yes, then congratulations on your sale! If you answered no to any of these questions, you have not yet sold your home.

I will contact you soon to find out how you scored and to show you how [UR Home Realty] can sell your home without any cost to you.

Yours truly,

_____

Enclosure: ← Card

Note: "Without any cost to you" would be explained in that your fee actually comes out of the buyer's pocket. It is part of the buyer's price. Buyers understand that it is their money that pays brokerage fees, and when buying direct from an owner, they expect the price to be reduced by the amount of the fee.

Use reverse directories to obtain owners' names from addresses or telephone numbers. You can also locate an owner from the office of your tax assessor or your local title company. Never address a letter "To Occupant"!

For-Sale-by-Owner Listing #2

UR

H O M E   R E A L T Y

_____ ← Date and address

_____
_____
_____

Dear _____:

If I had a full-price buyer for your home, would you be willing to pay our fee? Please call me if your answer is yes!

Yours truly,

_____

Enclosure: ← Card

Note: This short note will generally result in owner interest. It provides a chance to be invited to view the premises and to talk to the owner. You have not said you have a buyer; you only ask whether the owner would pay a fee if you had one. Chances are you will be working with several potential buyers who might be interested in the home. Agreeing to pay a fee to a particular buyer is just one step away from agreeing to pay a fee for any buyer.

This letter can be used for expired listings as well as for-sale-by-owner listings.

For-Sale-by-Owner Listing #3

UR
H O M E   R E A L T Y

_____ ← Date and address

_____
_____
_____

Dear _____:

I believe your home at [1821 High Street] will meet the needs of a [young family] that I [am working with] in their search for a new home. [They have a son, age 11, and a daughter, age 9,] and particularly desire [a colonial home within the Wilson School District], such as your home.

[1. Please call me   2. I will be stopping by] so that we can discuss their needs and ascertain whether your home is likely to be of interest to them.

Yours truly,

_____

Enclosure: ← Card

Note: Always use a real family you are working with who are likely to be interested in the house. The owners will probably try to sell you on their house and will be receptive to a short-term listing to accommodate your particular buyer. If your buyer is not interested in the house, the owners will generally be more receptive to a longer-term exclusive listing than they would have been had they not signed a listing with you already.

If you are acting as a buyer agent and will not be attempting seller representation, then you may call the owner even if that owner is listed on the do-not-call registry. You can call to arrange to show the home but not to solicit business.

For-Sale-by-Owner Listing #4

UR
H O M E   R E A L T Y

_____ ← Date and address

_____
_____
_____

Dear _____:

Why Do For-Sale-by-Owner Signs Get Replaced by Agent Signs?
Because Agents Sell!

Utilizing a real estate agent means the following:

- You are protected against unscrupulous buyers hoping to pay less than market value for your home.

- No unescorted, unqualified persons will enter your home.

- Contracts are likely to end in a sale—not in a courtroom.

- You are able to meet buyer financing needs.

- You are no longer a prisoner in your own home waiting for the bell to ring.

- You are more likely to sell your home.

- The sale will likely result in higher net proceeds.

Please think about it. I will stop by your home at [2:00 PM this Saturday] to answer any of your questions and to prove that everything I have told you is true. If this time is not convenient, please call me so I can arrange a more convenient time.

Yours truly,

_____

Enclosure: ← Card

Note: The approach that the owners can expect you at their door at a particular time forces the owners to consider your message. It can also result in a telephone contact initiated by the owners. While this approach is not for every salesperson and might result in some antagonistic owners, some agents have used it effectively with owners on the do-not-call registry.

For-Sale-by-Owner Listing #5

UR
H O M E   R E A L T Y

_____ ← Date and address

_____
_____
_____

Dear _____:

You probably know that

No Agent = No Commission

That seems like a good reason to try to sell without an agent, except that no agent all too often means no sale. That explains why agent signs replace so many for-sale-by-owner signs.

I will call on you at [2:00 PM this Saturday] to show you not only the positive benefits I can offer but also the dangers of owner sales. If I can show you how I can put more money in your pockets, will you want to talk with me?

Looking forward to seeing you,

_____

Enclosure: ← Card

Note: Telling owners you will be coming to their home is a strong approach that might create a negative reaction in some owners.

When you call on owners, reference your letter and ask, "Would it be all right if I took a look at your home?" or "Would you be offended if I asked to take a look at your home?" This type of an approach will likely give you an opportunity to tour the property and comment about positive features.

For-Sale-by-Owner Listing #6

UR
HOME REALTY

_____ ← Date and address

_____
_____
_____

Dear _____:

Can You Use Some Free Help?

Our office supplies [1. purchase offer forms 2. for-sale-by-owner signs 3. for-sale-by-owner suggestions] to owners who wish to sell their homes without using an agent. We do so without cost or obligation. We also provide a free estimate of value and recommended price based on current documented sales.

No, we are not a charity—we do this hoping that if you later decide to use an agent's services, you will remember our assistance.

Please call to set up an appointment so I can drop off the forms and explain how to use them and answer any questions you might have.

Yours truly,

_____

Enclosure: ← Card

Note: The free offer is an effective door opener. By explaining how the forms are to be filled out, with appropriate warnings, mandatory disclosures, applications for financing, qualifying ratios, FICO scores, and so on, the owner will begin to understand that selling a home is more complicated than just finding a buyer. You should then be in a position to discuss the benefits of having professional representation.

For-Sale-by-Owner Listing #7

UR
HOME REALTY

_____ ← Date and address

_____

_____

_____

Dear _____:

SOLD!

Is this the sign in front of your home? Or is it simply

For Sale by Owner?

The likelihood of turning the second sign into the first sign is very slim, which explains why brokers' signs replace so many for-sale-by-owner signs.

Facts:

1. Most calls on for-sale-by-owner signs come from people who can't afford the home they are calling about.
2. Most calls from newspaper ads are from people who would not be satisfied with a home priced in the range they inquired about.

Without having a variety of homes to match inquiries, most of an owner's efforts end up wasted and precious days will be lost.

I will contact you in the next few days, not to try to saddle you with an agent's selling fees but to show you how I can help you have more money in your pocket after a sale.

Isn't what you actually net more important than anything else?

Yours truly,

_____

Enclosure: ← Card

For-Sale-by-Owner Listing #8

UR
H O M E   R E A L T Y

_____ ← Date and address

_____
_____
_____

Dear _____:

Are you

Selling Without an Agent?
You Can Do It, but BE CAREFUL!

I have enclosed helpful hints and warnings that we have compiled to help owners who don't wish to use an agent. Study them carefully. Not only can they mean the difference between a sale and no sale, but they can also protect you against a lawsuit or the loss of your home to an unscrupulous buyer.

If you want an explanation of any of this material or would like to know how you might benefit financially and emotionally from being represented by an agent, please contact me.

I will check with you in a few days to see how you are doing and to offer whatever advice I can.

Yours truly,

_____

Enclosure: ← "How to Sell Without an Agent" can be adapted as an enclosure (see page 62).

Note: Weekend afternoons are a good time to contact for sale by owners (FSBO) who are trying to sell their homes because they are often at home hoping a buyer will contact them.

How to Sell Without an Agent

___

UR
HOME REALTY

_____ ← Date and address

_____
_____
_____

Dear _____:

Here's some help on

How to Sell Your Home Without an Agent

1. **Change ads regularly.** Ads lose their effectiveness if repeated without change. Three days is plenty for one ad. Rewrite ads to appeal to different categories of likely buyers. Use plenty of adjectives. Spend time writing good copy because your ad competes with many ads for similar property.

2. **Obtain purchase contract forms.** [Call our office if you do not have any.] Complete the purchase contract except for date, price, terms, and signatures. Make certain that you fully understand every provision. If a prospective buyer wants to provide the contract, be alert. Take it to an attorney. What appears to be a standard form might be one-sided and not say what it appears to say at first reading. With desktop publishing, many wheeler-dealers are using their own forms where the small print taketh away what the large print giveth!

3. **Check financing at least once a week with a mortgage company so you will be able to help a buyer understand down payment and monthly costs for various types of mortgages tailored to the buyer's needs.** Be prepared to explain loan types to prospective buyers. Many excellent texts are available to help you. You should also understand front-end and back-end qualifying ratios and FICO scores. If you don't understand them, you could waste days, weeks, or even months of effort on a buyer who is unable to obtain financing because of existing debt, insufficient income, or prior credit problems.

(1)

(2)

4. **If a prospective buyer uses the words "subordinate" or "subordination" in the offer, turn and run.** If you sign, no matter how good it looks, you are likely giving away your home to a sharp operator. Also, be alert for any deals that seem too good to be true—they generally are. Be particularly wary of buyers who are buying without any of their own cash. If buyers end up with more cash than they started with, you can be certain you are the victim of a scam. Television infomercials feature buyers who brag about paying practically nothing to own valuable property. A number of fast-talking seminar promoters have instructed thousands in unethical and often illegal procedures. Offers of mortgages on other property, notes, colored stones, diamonds (especially uncut), or other claimed valuables should send you running to an attorney. If you don't have one, I would be happy to recommend several. When an agent is involved, the fast operators don't waste their time. That's why they love for sale by owners.

5. **Be certain that you have considered and fully understand the effects of the following:** seller discount points, payoff penalties on existing loans, assumability of loans, ownership of the impound account, and all closing costs and who pays what.

6. **Make certain that you are prepared with all seller disclosures mandated by state law.** If you are not prepared, you may not be able to obligate a buyer to a sale; and if you fail to make a proper disclosure, you could be inviting a lawsuit and substantial damages.

7. **Make certain that you fully understand the requirements of state and federal fair housing legislation,** or you could find yourself paying a fine or a penalty.

8. **Make certain you know who a prospective buyer is before that person crosses your threshold.** There have been far too many horror stories of trusting homeowners who open their homes to persons with intentions other than buying. Try not to be alone when prospective buyers visit. Be particularly alert when couples separate while in your home.

9. **Beware of contingent offers.** As a result of a contingency, the property might be tied up for months or even years. The buyer could be a dealer who wants to hold the property as though it were an option to be exercised only if another buyer is located.

10. **Understand fully the tax consequences of the sale.** How much, if any, of the sales price will be subject to taxation, and at what rate?

---

(3)

If you are determined to sell your home yourself, we wish you good luck. I will, however, [1. be contacting you in the next few days 2. look forward to your call] to discuss some of the advantages of having agency representation that you may not have considered.

Yours truly,

_____

Enclosure: ← Card

Note: This letter can also be adapted as a handout or as an enclosure with other for-sale-by-owner letters. Even though the letter is long, it will be read because it appears to be offering benefits.

No-Cost Market Analysis Certificate

Free Market Analysis

This certificate is good for one free electronic comparative market analysis indicating the sales price you might expect to receive for your home in today's marketplace.

This analysis is provided without any charge or obligation on your part to list or sell your home.

[Bob Jones]   [602-555-8200]
[UR Home Realty]   Evenings: [602-555-6173]

Note: This certificate can be mailed to for-sale-by-owner families, as well as to potential clients in general. It can also be used as an enclosure, flyer, door hanger, or postcard.

Unsuccessful Listing Attempt

UR
H O M E   R E A L T Y

_____ ← Date and address

_____
_____
_____

Dear _____:

Thank you very much for the opportunity to visit your home in [Westwood]. I believe that [UR Home Realty] can help you find the perfect family who will appreciate all your home has to offer.

I will be contacting you again in a few weeks to give you an update on market conditions to help you analyze your marketing efforts and choose a plan for success.

Yours truly,

_____

Enclosure: ← Card

Note: A good time for a personal follow-up contact is late in the afternoon after the owner has had an open house.

RESPONSES TO OWNER INQUIRIES

Owner inquiries that can lead to listings should elicit a priority response. If a face-to-face or phone response is not practical, you should consider an e-mail response. There will be times when a party can be reached only by letter or desires a letter response. In such cases, consider an overnight delivery service such as FedEx.

Many of these e-mails can be used for a letter or a fax response. If so used, you should clearly indicate in the subject that you are supplying information that was requested.

If an inquiry is by letter, consider a phone call to obtain the party's e-mail address in order to meet the writer's request in a timely manner.

Response to Value Inquiry (Out-of-Area Owner) #1

To:

From: [agent@urhome.com]

Subject: Requested Value Analysis of [Elm Drive] Property

Attachment(s):   Comparative Market Analysis—Agency Agreement

Dear _____:

Regarding your inquiry about the value of your [1. lot 2. home 3. building] at [1847 Elm Drive], the current market indications would support a sales price in the [$350,000] to [$375,000] range.

[1. This value is based on (the present excellent condition of your property, its size, age, location, and amenities,) and the recent sale of the following:]

[1411 Elm Drive]	[$359,000]	[Similar size, age, and location]
[2114 Cedar Drive]	[$372,000]	[Same age, floor plan, and builder]
[1821 Cedar Drive]	[$349,500]	[Very similar except only a 2-car garage]

[2. The value is based on the attached comparative market analysis and the fact that your (home) has (list features influencing value).]

Because of the current market conditions, I recommend a list price of [$379,000] and I have attached an agency agreement reflecting this price. Please endorse and fax or e-mail a signed copy to our office so we can begin our efforts to obtain a buyer for your [1. lot 2. home 3. building].

Yours truly,

_____

Note: Do not give out information concerning sales without the permission of buyers and sellers. Multiple listing service (MLS) agreements generally give permission. Never give a value estimate without carefully checking the property and recent comparable sales.

The positive features should show that you appreciate the property's benefits. Don't be picky about the negative features, but list some of them when you are certain that the owner realizes they are present.

The last paragraph assumes that the owner will list the property. By reading this assumption and the instructions, owners often comply.

If possible, the letter should be followed by a phone call to ascertain whether the owner has any questions.

Because the owner contacted you, the do-not-call rules do not apply.

Instructions with the agency agreement should be to return it by fax, by first scanning it and then attaching it to an e-mail, or by mailing.

If the party is in the area, call to personally deliver the comparative market analysis and continue with a listing presentation. A letter or e-mail should only be used for owners who are out of the area.

Response to Value Inquiry (Out-of-Area Owner) #2

To:	
From:	[agent@urhome.com]
Subject:	Requested Value Analysis of [Midvale Lane] Property
Attachment(s):	Comparative Market Analysis—Seller's Net Proceeds—Agency Agreement

Dear _____:

In response to your inquiry about the value of your property at [I I I Midvale Lane], I have performed a comparative market analysis. The analysis shows similar properties recently sold, similar properties currently on the market, and similar properties not sold at their listed prices. Based on the enclosed comparative market analysis, I recommend that your property be placed on the market at [$475,000]. I have also included agency agreements reflecting this price.

I believe it is a particularly advantageous time to place your property on the market because of [1. the increase in sales activity 2. the opportunity to lock in the recent appreciation in value 3. the current low interest rates 4. the increasing demand for homes in the area]. Please endorse and fax the agency agreement, and we will immediately get to work on marketing your [1. home 2. property].

I will be calling you to answer any questions that you might have.

Yours truly,

_____

Note: The term "agency agreement" has a benefit connotation. "Listing" often has a negative connotation because the word is associated with commission rather than with benefits. See the notes in previous letter.

Response to Value Inquiry (Out-of-Area Owner) #3

To:

From: [agent@urhome.com]

Subject: Requested Net Proceeds from Sale of [Hampton Road] Property

Attachment(s):   Comparative Market Analysis—Agency Agreement

Dear _____:

You wanted to know what you should be able to net from a sale of your [Hampton Road property] after paying off your loan and all sales-related expenses.

The answer is [$146,000] cash. That is our current best estimate of what you will have after paying off the mortgage and all sales and closing costs for a sale of your home at [28146 Hampton Road].

This estimate is based on the enclosed comparative market analysis indicating that your home should sell for [$349,000]. The enclosed seller's proceeds estimate shows the estimated deductions from the gross sales price to arrive at the net.

I have attached agency agreements reflecting the [$349,000] sale price. If [$146,000] cash interests you, please endorse and fax the agreements to our office so we can immediately get to work on selling your home.

I will be calling you to answer any questions that you might have.

Yours truly,

_____

Note: Like the previous two letters, a value inquiry should be answered by e-mail or mail only when the owner is not available for a personal presentation.

Response to Value Inquiry—Poor Market Conditions

To:

From: [agent@urhome.com]

Subject: Requested Market Analysis for [Lemon Court] property

Attachment(s):   Comparative Market Analysis—Agency Agreement

Dear _____:

At present, the number of sellers far exceeds the number of buyers for [1. lots
2. houses   3. office buildings]. Figures from the [Inland Board of REALTORS®] indicate
that only [19 percent] of the [1. lots   2. houses   3. office buildings] listed for sale in
the [Bloomington] area sold within [90] days of listing.

Similar properties are currently listed between [$430,000] and [$490,000], but they
are not generating much buyer interest at these prices. When properties have sold,
their sale prices have generally been significantly lower than the prices at which the
properties were listed. The enclosed comparative market analysis confirms this. This
does not mean that we cannot sell your [home at 3817 Midvale Circle]. In fact, I am
optimistic about its salability, provided we give your [home] a competitive edge. A
list price of [$409,000], which you can see is in line with the actual sale prices of
similar [homes], will attract buyer attention and is likely to result in a sale even under
our present market conditions.

I have enclosed an agency agreement for your property reflecting the above price.
Please endorse and fax or e-mail a signed copy. I will be calling you in a few days to
answer any questions that you might have.

Yours truly,

_____

Note: When most listings expire unsold, this letter's strength is its honesty. It will be a
salable listing if you get it—not one likely to cost you money.

Response to Value Inquiry—Repairs Needed

To:

From: [agent@urhome.com]

Subject: Requested Market Analysis for [Midvale Circle] property

Attachment(s):   Comparative Market Analysis—Agency Agreement

Dear _____:

I have carefully examined your home at [381 Lemon Court]. The resulting comparative market analysis is enclosed.

While I am confident that I will be able to find a buyer at the price indicated in my analysis, you should seriously consider some property repairs.

The work I recommend consists of the following:

- [Paint the exterior.]
- [Repair the porch and railing.]
- [Paint the entryway, living room, and kitchen in light colors.]
- [Install a new lighting fixture in kitchen.]
- [Replace the floor tile in the bath.]
- [Professionally clean the carpets.]

Based on [1. an enclosed estimate from Harkin Home Maintenance 2. my experience in handling similar repair work], the total cost should be about [$2,500].

From the comparative market analysis, you will see that these repairs should result in an increase of [$5,500] in the selling price.

I would be happy to assist you in obtaining firm bids for all the work and also to assist you in securing any desired financing.

I have enclosed an agency agreement for the property based on selling the property without any repairs. Please endorse and fax or e-mail the agreement. If you decide to go ahead with the repairs and improvements, we can adjust the price to reflect the improvements.

I will be calling you to answer any questions that you might have.

Yours truly,

Note: The choice is not whether to endorse a listing, but whether to make repairs or sell the property "as is."

Again, a letter such as this should be used only when a personal presentation is not possible.

Response to Value Inquiry—
Apartment Listing and Management

To:	
From:	[agent@urhome.com]
Subject:	Requested Market Analysis for [Jackson Street Apartments]
Attachment(s):	Comparative Market Analysis—Management Agreement—Agency Agreement

Dear _____:

I have completed an in-depth analysis of your apartment building at [11476 Jackson Street]. The enclosed comparative market analysis is based on the following:

1. [Raising the rents of units one, three, and seven by an additional $120 per month and raising the rents of units four, six, eight, and ten by $80 per month. These rents are currently below market rents for comparable (Eastside) units.]

2. [Painting vacant units five and nine, as well as replacing the carpeting]

3. [Painting the entry hall and replacing all carpeting in public areas]

4. [Painting the exterior and performing needed landscaping work, including planting flowers]

We would be happy to take charge of all required work. Enclosed is a property management agreement, as well as an agency agreement. Please endorse and return a faxed copy of each so that we can immediately start preparing your property for a favorable sale.

I will contact you within the next few days to answer any questions that you might have, or you may call me at [602-555-8200].

Yours truly,

_____

Note: When you sell apartments, having management authority will allow you to make the property more salable and increase your likelihood of success.

Response About Our Firm (Out-of-Area Inquiry)

To:	
From:	[agent@urhome.com]
Subject:	Requested Information About URHome Realty and Property Analysis
Attachment(s):	Comparative Market Analysis—Agency Agreement

Dear _____:

In answer to your inquiry about [UR Home Realty], I would like to tell you about our firm.

[We have served the real estate needs in (Anderson County) for (26 years).] [I have been engaged in the real estate business since (1985).] [1. We are one of the largest firms in the area, with (56) salespeople in (three) offices. 2. We are a small firm specializing in (suburban residential property).]

[As a member in good standing of the (Pineview) Multiple Listing Service, we are able to make your home available to (118) offices and more than (600) salespeople. Our success record has been exemplary over the past few years, and (based on our present record,) I expect continued success for the future.]

For more information about [UR Home Realty as well as testimonial letters from buyers and sellers], I hope you will check our Web site: [www.urhome.com].

I have attached a comparative market analysis prepared for your home, showing what you could expect to receive at a sale. Also attached is an agency agreement reflecting our recommended sale price. Please fax a signed copy of the agreement to us.

I will be calling you to answer any questions you may have.

Yours truly,

_____

Note: Personal contact is always preferable to an e-mail or letter.

Response to Inquiry About Firm

<table>
<tr><td align="right">To:</td><td></td></tr>
<tr><td align="right">From:</td><td>[agent@urhome.com]</td></tr>
<tr><td align="right">Subject:</td><td>Information About [UR Home Realty]</td></tr>
<tr><td align="right">Attachment(s):</td><td>Resume Information About UR Home Realty, [How We Market], and [Client Benefits]</td></tr>
</table>

Dear _____:

Your interest in [UR Home Realty] is greatly appreciated. I have enclosed a brief personal résumé, information about our firm, and [1. information about how we successfully market property and the benefits you will receive by having our firm represent you. 2. reasons buyers should have their own representatives and the benefits our firm can provide for you].

I will be contacting you to answer any questions you may have. You can expect our best efforts in meeting your personal needs.

Yours truly,

_____

Referral of Inquiry

UR
HOME REALTY

_____ ← Date and address

_____
_____
_____

Dear _____:

I appreciate your considering [UR Home Realty] for marketing your property at [48141 Calhoun Road].

Because [1. we limit our activity to Sun City 2. we do not handle commercial property 3. we do not have a property management department], I have referred your inquiry to [Lynn Jones] at [Jones Realty]. [Lynn (1. devotes her efforts to the Mayville area 2. specializes in commercial property 3. specializes in property management and has the prestigious certified property manager (CPM) designation).] [Lynn] will be contacting you in the next few days. [Lynn] can be contacted at [747-206-7656 or e-mail LynnJ@hotmail.com.]

[1. We have successfully referred (1. buyers and sellers 2. persons in need of property management) to (Lynn Jones) in the past and feel certain that (she) will be able to help you. 2. (Jones Realty) is a member of (Refer-All, Inc.), the referral service to which we belong. Because the members are all trained professionals, I feel certain that they will be able to help you.]

Again, thank you for considering [UR Home Realty]. If we can serve you in the future, please feel free to contact me at [602-555-8200].

Yours truly,

_____

Enclosure: ← Card

Note: This letter treats a value inquiry as an offer of a listing. It increases the likelihood that the referral firm will be able to obtain an agency agreement.

A letter is preferable to an e-mail in this situation because it is personal and shows consideration. Consider sending letter by FedEx or other priority mail method.

Refusal of Open Listing

To:

From: [agent@urhome.com]

Subject: Reply to Agency Offer

Attachment(s):   Agency Agreement

Dear _____:

Thank you very much for offering our firm an open listing on your property at [8669 Norbert Way]. We must, however, decline your kind offer. Our acceptance of an open listing would not be fair to you.

Experience has shown that property that is not listed exclusively will generally remain unsold. The open listing will likely be shown only when an agent doesn't have an exclusive agency property to fit a buyer's needs. Accepting such a listing would give you false hope for sales success.

I have therefore attached an exclusive-right-to-sell agency agreement making [UR Home Realty] responsible for selling your [home]. If you are serious about wishing to sell, please endorse and fax or e-mail a copy of the agreement.

I will be calling you to answer any questions and to tell you about our marketing plan for your [home].

Yours truly,

_____

Note: This e-mail is for an owner who lives outside the area. Otherwise, personal contact should be made. You may also wish to include a comparative market analysis. To many, the term "agency agreement" creates an image of a helpful partnership, while the word "listing" carries a more negative connotation.

RESIDENTIAL BUYER SOLICITATIONS

If you send an unsolicited e-mail, include your physical address as well as an opt-out mechanism, such as the following:

☐ Please do not send me any further e-mails about real estate opportunities.

Letter to Renter #1

UR

H O M E   R E A L T Y

_____ ← Date and address

_____
_____
_____

Dear _____:

Tired of Renting?

■ Would you like to enjoy the privacy of your own home?

■ Would you like affordable home payments?

■ Would you like home equity rather than rent receipts?

■ Would you like the security of ownership?

Do you want to find out how you can be an owner—rather than a renter—with a down payment and monthly payments tailored to your individual needs?

Call me at [602-555-8200] or send an e-mail to [agent@urhome.com] now for a no-obligation homebuyer analysis that can mean an end to rent receipts.

Yours truly,

_____

Enclosure: ← Card

Note: This letter, as well as others in this section, is directed toward turning tenants into owners. For mailings, we suggest using a reverse directory to target apartment dwellers. Letters to units that have many younger families will be especially productive.

An additional enclosure can be a sheet showing photos of several homes without any information other than a statement such as "No down payment needed" or "5% down will make it yours."

Letter to Renter #2

UR
H O M E   R E A L T Y

_____ ← Date and address

_____
_____
_____

Dear _____ :

Want to

Escape the Landlord?

If you're tired of collecting rent receipts and would like to have something for your money, I have homes for you with the following amenities:

- ▓ Very low or possibly no down payment
- ▓ Monthly payments similar to rent
- ▓ Three and even four bedrooms
- ▓ Your own [double] garage
- ▓ Your own [fenced] backyard

Call me at [602-555-8200] today or send an e-mail to [agent@urhome.com] and say goodbye to your landlord.

Yours truly,

_____

Enclosure: ← Card

Note: See the note on the previous letter.

Letter to Renter #3

UR
H O M E   R E A L T Y

_____ ← Date and address

_____
_____
_____

Dear _____:

Do you

Love Your Landlord?

I bet your landlord loves you. Your landlord gets the rent and tax deductions, and you get rent receipts. That's a pretty good deal—for your landlord.

Kiss Your Landlord Goodbye

A low-down-payment or a possible no-down-payment loan can put you in your own home by [Labor Day]. All you have to do is call [602-555-8200].

Yours truly,

_____

Enclosure: ← Card

Note: See the note on previous letters.

Tenant Solicitation

UR

H O M E   R E A L T Y

_____ ← Date and address

_____
_____
_____

Dear _____:

Before we advertise to the general public, we would like to give you the first opportunity to purchase the home at [8847 Highland, the white house just down the street from where you are renting]. It has just been placed on the market.

Call me now at [602-555-8200] for additional information and to discuss advantageous financing arrangements. Incidentally, we also have some other very interesting properties available.

Yours truly,

_____

Enclosure: ← Card, photographs of home

Note: This letter gives very little information, but it makes the tenant think of the possibility of becoming an owner.

Offer to Qualify for a Loan

UR
H O M E   R E A L T Y

_____ ← Date and address

_____
_____
_____

Dear _____:

Can You Afford to Buy a Home?

With current low interest rates [and a depressed market], chances are that not only can you become a homeowner, but you also may qualify for a much finer home than you believed possible.

Free Loan Qualifying Analysis

Allow me to prepare, at no cost or obligation to you, a homebuyer qualifying analysis. This analysis will show you how much you can afford to finance under a variety of available loans, including some having no down payments and very low down payments. To obtain this personal home purchase qualifying analysis, all you have to do is call [602-555-8200].

Yours truly,

_____

Enclosure: ← Card

Note: This is an excellent approach for young families who are renting.

Home Buying Seminar—Free

HOME REALTY

Home Buying Seminar

Many seminars charge hundreds of dollars to learn how to buy homes with low or even no down payment. [UR Home Realty] will show you how and a great deal more without cost or obligation.

The seminar includes the following:

- How to search the local market on your home computer
- How to buy with low down or even no down payment
- How large a loan you can obtain
- What type of loan best meets your needs
- Tax benefits of being a home owner
- What your total monthly housing costs will be
- Obtaining a preapproval for a loan
- [The difference between using a seller's agent or having your own agent to help you search for your perfect home]

[Thursday, October 4, at 7:00 PM]

[UR Home Realty]

[2734 East 24th Street]

[Eureka]

[Please RSVP 602-555-8200. Seating is limited.]

Note: This flyer can be distributed in rental areas and included as an enclosure to other letters.

Marriage or Engagement

UR
H O M E   R E A L T Y

_____ ← Date and address

_____
_____
_____

Dear _____:

Congratulations on your recent [1. marriage 2. engagement]!

Need assistance in meeting any present or future housing needs? We have [rentals ranging from ($400) to ($4,000) a month and] homes that can be purchased with a low and possibly even no down payment with financing tailored to your particular needs.

I would like to offer you a housing consultation with no cost or obligation to you. This includes a needs analysis, market analysis, and no obligation prequalification for a housing loan if you decide to make a purchase. Please call me at [602-555-8200] if you would like to take advantage of this offer.

Yours truly,

_____

Enclosure: ← Card

Note: The social pages of your local papers, as well as church bulletins, will provide the information you need. Local church bulletins may be available on the Internet for ready access.

New Parents #1

UR
HOME REALTY

_____ ← Date and address

_____
_____
_____

Dear _____:

Congratulations on your new [1. son   2. daughter]!

Although I won't help out with the 2:00 AM feeding or the diapers, I can help you if you need more family space.

We have an unusually good selection of family homes, many of which allow flexible financing to meet individual buyers' needs. [Even a no down payment loan is possible.]

Call me at [602-555-8200] to see how easy it can be to own your own single-family home with a [child-safe, fenced] backyard that is all yours.

Yours truly,

_____

Enclosure: ← Card

Note: Birth announcements in newspapers are particularly effective for targeting addresses of families who are living in apartments, condominiums, or manufactured homes.

New Parents #2

UR

H O M E   R E A L T Y

_____ ← Date and address

_____
_____
_____

Dear _____ :

Congratulations on the birth of your [1. son (John) 2. daughter (Mary Jane)]! It won't be long before [1. he 2. she] will be running around in seemingly perpetual motion. Now is the time to consider a home with your own backyard for [1. John 2. Mary Jane].

We presently have some great low- and possibly even no-down-payment opportunities. We can also help you prequalify for a home loan so that when you find the property you want to call your home, you can be ready to act.

Are you interested? [1. I will be calling you in the next few days to discuss your housing needs and provide financing information. 2. Call me today so I can determine your housing needs and explain the various financing options presently available.]

Yours truly,

_____

Enclosure: ← Card

Note: Birth announcements in newspapers are particularly effective for targeting addresses of families who are living in apartments, condominiums, or manufactured homes.
Check the do-not-call registry before you indicate that a call will be made. Lower-income apartment dwellers are less likely to be on the registry than higher-income homeowners.

New Parents #3

UR

H O M E   R E A L T Y

_____ ← Date and address

_____

_____

_____

Dear _____:

Congratulations on the birth of your [1. son (Jeffrey) 2. daughter (Mary Jane)].

If you stop by our office at [712 West Main Street] we have a little gift for you [1. six pair of colorful infant socks. 2. a fleece crib blanket].

Our very best to [1. John 2. Mary Jane] and [1. his 2. her] parents.

Sincerely,

_____

Enclosure: ← Card

Note: While the gift should be unconditional, you should ask the parents to fill out a short questionnaire:

Name: _____   E-mail: _____

Address: _____

- ▪ Type of residence   ☐ Home   ☐ Apartment   ☐ Condominium
  ☐ Manufactured home   ☐ Own   ☐ Rent

- ▪ How long have you lived at the present address? _____

- ▪ Does your present housing fit your current and future needs?   ☐ Yes   ☐ No

- ▪ Would you like a no-obligation analysis of financing available to you?
  ☐ Yes   ☐ No

- ▪ Would you like to receive e-mails about new listings?   ☐ Yes   ☐ No

- ▪ May we have permission to contact you by telephone about housing needs?
  ☐ Yes   ☐ No

Sign

Note: Baby gifts such as those mentioned can be purchased wholesale on the Internet for less than $5 each.

Offer to Aid in Tenant Relocation

UR
H O M E   R E A L T Y

_____ ← Date and address

_____

_____

_____

Dear _____:

I would like to offer my services to help you meet your relocation housing needs for rental or home purchase. [1. I will contact you in the next few days to tell you 2. Call me today if you want to learn] about low- and no-down-payment home purchase opportunities, as well as what is available in the local rental market.

Yours truly,

_____

Enclosure: ← Card

Note: This letter can be used when apartments are converted to cooperatives or condominiums, or when property is taken by eminent domain or razed for redevelopment. If the tenant is not on the do-not-call registry, use the phone for your contact.

Tenant Solicitation—Condominium Conversion

UR

H O M E   R E A L T Y

_____ ← Date and address

_____
_____
_____

Dear _____:

Because [John Jones], the owner of your apartment building, [1. is in the process of converting your building to condominiums 2. has received approval to convert your building's units to cooperatives], you have a rare opportunity.

As the tenant, you have the first opportunity to purchase your unit [1. with an exceptionally low down payment 2. at an attractive interest rate]. Besides being protected against future rent increases, you will be eligible for income tax deductions that will mean big savings to you. In addition, you, not the landlord, will benefit by any future appreciation in value of your unit.

I will stop by to see you [this Saturday afternoon] to explain various available financing options and to show you how easy it will be to go from tenant to owner.

Yours truly,

_____

Enclosure: ← Card

Note: The current tenants have three choices: (1) buy the unit they currently occupy, (2) buy somewhere else, or (3) find a new rental. Any of the available options presents an opportunity for an agent.

Letter to Neighbor After Residential Listing

UR
H O M E   R E A L T Y

_____ ← Date and address

_____
_____
_____

Dear _____:

Our office has recently listed the home of your neighbor [John Jones] at [322 Maple Lane] for sale. You have probably noticed our For Sale sign.

I am writing to ask for your help in locating a buyer for this fine home. In other words, you can help us find your new neighbor.

The home has [three bedrooms, two baths, and a den] [and, as you know, it has been lovingly cared for]. This great home is priced right, so anyone you suggest would be thankful for your recommendation. [1. I will be contacting you to see whether 2. Please contact me if] you can suggest any friends or acquaintances who might want to be your neighbor.

Thanking you in advance for your help,

_____

Enclosure: ← Card, property flyer

Note: Be certain to follow through by checking with the neighbors, if you indicate that you will do so. If neighbors are not listed on the do-not-call registry, then your contact can be by phone. If they are listed on the registry, you will have to visit them.

Letter to Former Residential Buyer

UR

H O M E   R E A L T Y

_____ ← Date and address

_____
_____
_____

Dear _____:

It has been [almost one year] since you moved into your new home in [Orchard Ridge]. I am certain you and your family are pleased with your purchase.

The reason I am writing you is that a home in your neighborhood has just come on the market. It is a [3-year-old, 3-bedroom, 2½-bath Spanish Ranch] at [9217 Westwood Place] priced at [$389,900].

I will be calling you in the next few days to see whether you can suggest any friends or acquaintances who might want to be your new neighbors.

Your friendly real estate agent,

_____

Enclosure: ← Card, property flyer

Note: Even if the recipient is on the do-not-call registry, you can call within 18 months of a completed transaction.

Open House—Invitation to a Neighbor

UR
HOME REALTY

_____ ← Date and address

_____
_____
_____

Dear _____:

I would like you to [1. be my guest for coffee and cake   2. visit with me] on

[Sunday, October 12]

[1:00 PM to 4:00 PM]

at the [1. Johnson residence   2. former Johnson residence], [7413 Lynwood Avenue].

You will be able to view this fine home, which we are proud to offer for sale. Please bring any friends who might be interested in becoming your new neighbor. I look forward to seeing you!

Yours truly,

_____

Enclosure: ← Card

Note: A similar invitation can be sent to prospective buyers with whom you have had prior contact.

Open House—Invitation to Previous Visitor

UR
HOME REALTY

_____ ← Date and address

_____
_____
_____

Dear _____:

You visited one of our open houses on [October 7] at [37 Westwood Lane] in [Orchard Ridge].

I want to tell you about [1. several other 2. an] open house[s] we will have [this coming Saturday and Sunday], [October 14 and 15], from [11:00 AM to 4:00 PM].

[1. 7112 Hiawatha Drive]

[A 2,500+ sq ft, 3-year-old Tuscany Mediterranean

with 3 bedrooms, den, and 2½ baths]

[$587,000]

[2. 3820 Thomas Circle]

[A 2,700 sq ft, 1-year-new New England Colonial

with 4 bedrooms, 3 baths, and a 4-car garage]

[$612,000]

If you are interested in a new home, you will definitely want to see [1. this home 2. these two homes]. I think that you will be delighted with the area, the special features offered, and the value.

[Bring this letter with you to redeem a special free gift!]

Yours truly,

_____

Enclosure: ← Card, photo(s)

Note: Letters such as this will increase open house traffic as well as show the owners that you are expending extra effort on their behalf. A free gift such as a baseball cap or a coffee mug with your firm's name on it will increase the effectiveness of the letter. If the open house visitor provided an e-mail address on the open house visitor rating (page 100), then an e-mail notification would be appropriate.

Open House—Visitor Rating Form

UR
HOME REALTY

Name: _____

Property: _____ Date: _____

Reason for visiting this open house: ☐ advertising ☐ signs
☐ other (specify): _____

Features I particularly like: _____
_____
_____

Features I do not like: _____
_____
_____

Features I want that this property does not have: _____
_____
_____

I believe the price offering is: ☐ low ☐ about right ☐ high

Do you presently own your home? _____

Is it currently listed for sale with an agent? _____

General comments: _____
_____
_____

I would like to receive: ☐ e-mail ☐ phone calls on new listings before they are
advertised to the general public.

I would like to be notified about future open houses by ☐ phone ☐ e-mail

Locations of interest: _____
_____

Special features desired: _____

Price range: _____ Phone number: _____

E-mail address: _____

Note: This is a form rather than a letter. It is designed to obtain useful information for listing and selling. Of course, you should relay information about the property to the owner.

By checking the appropriate boxes, the visitor is agreeing to contact by phone calls and/or e-mails on other properties. Many open-house viewers will be interested in receiving an e-mail of new listings before others know about them.

Notice of Model Home Tour

To:	
From:	[agent@urhome.com]
Subject:	Tour Model Homes on Sunday

Visit [6] New Developments in [Westwood] in a single day.

Homes priced from [$139,500 to $239,000] with

[Special Builder Incentives]

[Fantastic Financing]

[Sunday August 12]

[1:00 PM]

We leave by [bus] [van] [caravan] from

Our office at [111 Main Street].

Contact me by return e-mail

Or call [(602) 555-8200] to reserve your place.

Note: Your e-mail list would include visitors to other open houses, as well as your current prospects. If this e-mail is completely unsolicited, then you must include an opt-out mechanism.

Of course, you must coordinate the tour with developers who have agreed to cooperate.

Have handout material for each property. If you tour by caravan, have maps available.

Notice of Home Tour (Fixer-Uppers)

To:

From: [Agent@urhome.com]

Subject: Fixer-Upper Home Tour

[7] Fixer-Uppers in [Northridge] priced from

[$87,500 to $211,000] with [2 to 5] bedrooms and [1 ½ to 3] baths.

These homes have two things in common:

■ They need a lot of TLC.

■ They are bargain priced.

Tour them with us on

[Sunday, August 12, at 1:00 PM].

We leave by [bus] [van] [caravan]

from our office at [111 Main Street].

Contact me today by return e-mail to reserve your place [seating is limited].

[J Jones]

[UR Home Realty]

[602-555-8200]

Note: Have the owners' permission to market homes as fixer-uppers. Send this to prospects who have responded to fixer-upper ads or indicated interest in less than perfect properties, as well as to investors. Consider converting this e-mail to a classified ad to obtain a greater response. If unsolicited, the e-mail must include an opt-out mechanism.

Have handout material for each property. If you tour by caravan, have maps available.

Notice of Home Tour (Foreclosures)

To:

From: [agent@urhome.com]

Subject: Foreclosure Home Tour

Tour [9] Foreclosures in [Brookfield] available from the lenders at a fraction of original cost.

Now priced from [$139,500 to $179,500]

[Sunday, August 12, at 1:00 PM]

We leave by [bus] [van] [caravan]

From our office at [111 Main Street].

Contact me today by return e-mail

Or call [602-555-8200] to reserve your place [seating is limited].

[J Jones]

[UR Home Realty]

[602-555-8200]

Note: Use a prospect list, as well as open house visitor lists, for this e-mail. Also, consider tailoring this e-mail to use as a classified ad. Be certain to have information sheets available about each property. If you tour by caravan, have maps available. If this contact is unsolicited, an opt-out mechanism is required.

Notice of Home Tour (Short Sales)

To:	
From:	[agent@urhome.com]
Subject:	Short Sale Open House Tour

Question: What is a short sale?

Answer: A sale where the lender agrees to a sale price below what is owned on the property.

Your Benefit: A chance to buy a home at a fraction of what it formerly sold for.

Tour [5] Short Sales in [Westwood]

[Sunday, August 12 at 1:00 PM]

We leave by [bus] [van] [caravan]

From our office at [111 Main Street].

Contact me today by return e-mail

Or call [602-555-8200] to reserve your place [seating is limited].

[J Jones]

[UR Home Realty]

[602-555-8200]

Note: Use a prospect list, as well as open house visitor lists, for this e-mail. Also, consider tailoring this e-mail to use as a classified ad. If e-mail is unsolicited, an opt-out mechanism is required.
Be certain to have information sheets available about each property. If you tour by caravan, have maps available.

Open House—Thank You to Visitor

UR

HOME REALTY

_____ ← Date and address

_____
_____
_____

Dear _____:

I would like to thank you for visiting our firm's open house at [3714 Baxley Circle] [last weekend].

[I will be calling to ask you for your impression of the house and how it fits your needs.] I have enclosed information on several other available homes [as well as upcoming open houses]. If you are interested in any of them, I will be happy to arrange a showing.

Yours truly,

_____

Enclosure: ← Card, property information

Note: A thank you letter is more personal than an e-mail although an e-mail could be used. A letter saying you will call forces a person to think about the call and what to tell you. It is a power approach to letter writing. Do not call if the person is on the do-not-call registry and has not given permission to call (see permission authorization on Open House Visitor Rating Form on page 100).

Notice of Sale to Open House Visitor

UR
H O M E   R E A L T Y

_____ ← Date and address

_____
_____
_____

Dear _____:

The open house you recently viewed at [69142 Sunrise Canyon Road] has just been sold. However, we have recently received several very attractive new listings that I feel will be of great interest to you. I have enclosed information on several of these fine homes. You can view additional offerings [including virtual tours] by visiting our Web site at [www.urhome.com and clicking on the box "Homes for Sale"].

I feel certain that I can find the perfect home for you as to size, location, price, and terms. [1. I will call you in the next few days to determine your specific housing needs so that I can begin to work for you. 2. Please call me so I can begin working to fulfill your housing needs.]

Yours truly,

_____

Enclosure: ← Card, property information

Note: A letter saying you will call forces a person to think about the call and what to tell you. It is a power approach to letter writing. If the visitor provided an e-mail address, an e-mail would be appropriate. Do not call if the person is on the do-not-call registry and has not given permission to call (see permission authorization on Open House Visitor Rating Form on page 100).

Chamber of Commerce Inquiry

UR
H O M E   R E A L T Y

_____ ← Date and address

_____
_____
_____

Dear _____:

The [Midvale] Chamber of Commerce has indicated that you are considering becoming one of our neighbors.

Perhaps I am a bit premature, but I would like to welcome you to our community and offer you our relocation assistance. I would be happy to arrange motel reservations when you visit the area. If you desire any specific information, let me know.

I am including some general information about several of our housing opportunities. I have also enclosed a Housing Needs Checklist, which will help me in meeting your specific needs.

I suggest you check our Web site, [www.urhome.com]. You can review the housing inventory presently available [and even take virtual tours through many of the properties].

Call me at [800-555-1 1 1 1] for any additional information you would like.

Yours truly,

_____

Enclosure: ← Card, property information, Housing Needs Checklist

Note: See the Housing Needs Checklist on page 109. Having an office or personal 800 number greatly increases the likelihood of receiving a call. If the person is not listed on the do-not-call registry, a follow-up call should be made.

If the party provided an e-mail address, then this letter could easily be tailored for an e-mail response.

Housing Needs Checklist

UR
HOME REALTY

Housing Needs Checklist

Presently I   ☐ own a home ☐ rent

☐ I must sell before I relocate

☐ My home is currently listed for sale

I prefer to   ☐ rent   ☐ purchase

I prefer a(n)   ☐ single-family home   ☐ condominium   ☐ apartment

Estimated rental range: $ _____ to $ _____

Estimated purchase price:
☐ Under $100,000

☐ $100,000–$150,000

☐ $150,000–$200,000

☐ $200,000–$300,000

☐ $300,000–$450,000

☐ $450,000–$700,000

☐ Over $700,000

Size of family: _____

Names and ages of children: _____; _____;
_____; _____; _____

Pets: _____

Number of bedrooms desired: _____

Number of baths desired: _____

Particular locations I am interested in (if known): _____
_____

Required special features (disability, pets, hobbies, etc.): _____
_____

(1)

---

(2)

I expect to be:
   Checking the area around (date) _____
   Relocating around (date) _____

☐ I would like to receive e-mails of new listings that appear to meet my requirements before the listings are advertised to the general public.

Name: _____

Address: _____

Phone: _____

E-mail: _____

Note: This checklist can be used as an enclosure with the answer to any inquiry about property (letter or e-mail). The price range might need to be adjusted to reflect your local market.
If mailed, a self-addressed stamped envelope should be included.

Out-of-Area Buyer Inquiry—Buyer Agency Solicitation

UR
H O M E   R E A L T Y

_____ ← Date and address

_____
_____
_____

Dear _____:

I have [1. e-mailed   2. included] information you requested about [present available properties in (Westport Heights)].

Because agents whose duties are to get the best deal possible for the seller represent sellers, buyers need to have someone who will be primarily concerned with their interests.

I am a buyer's agent. I like to work with just a few buyers at a time so I can devote all my efforts to meeting their needs.

While you might not have considered having your own agent, some of the advantages are as follows:

- I will help you separate and prioritize needs and wants.

- I will help you prequalify for a loan so that any offer you make will be from a position of strength.

- I will locate property available for purchase, including property not available through seller's agents, which might include lender-owned property, property in foreclosure or probate, and even property for sale by owner.

- I will not waste your time viewing unsuitable property by showing you property to please an owner or because it is my own listing.

- I will analyze locations as to their desirability in relation to your specific needs and interests.

- Prior to any offer, I will prepare a comparative market analysis to determine the fair value range of the property. A price asked by a seller might bear little relationship to actual value.

(1)

(2)

- Before you sign anything, I will make certain that you fully understand your financial obligations.

- I will make purchase recommendations as to property, as well as the price to be offered, with the goal of obtaining the property that suits you best at the lowest price; of course, all decisions will be yours.

- I will use my experience to protect you against unfair contracts including seller fraud.

- I will advise you throughout the negotiating process.

- I will make certain the property is as represented by recommending an inspection by a qualified home inspector.

- I will explain various financing options and types of loans available and will recommend loan types and lenders based solely on your best interests and not on any personal interest on my part.

- I will help and advise you throughout the financing process.

- I will monitor the closing process to make certain everything is accomplished as agreed.

What Does Agency Cost You?

In most cases, nothing. When the seller has listed with an agent, which is the case in most sales, my fee is paid out of the seller's pocket, not yours.

I have enclosed an agency agreement. By signing and returning [three] copies, you can have your own agent working for you. I will be calling you to answer any questions you may have. To find out more about [UR Home Realty] and me, visit our Web site at [www.urhome.com].

Yours truly,

_____

Enclosure: ← Card, agency agreement, self-addressed stamped envelope.

Note: While the letter is long, a list format will encourage the recipient to read it in full.

Buyer Agency Flyer

How Can Buyers Protect Themselves?

Did you know that the real estate agent who advertises a property, shows the property to a buyer, helps the buyer make decisions, and prepares the purchase offer doesn't necessarily have the buyer's best interests in mind? That's right, the helpful agent might be the exclusive agent of the seller with agency duties to get the best deal possible for the seller with no agency duties whatsoever to the buyer.

As a buyer, you can protect yourself by having a buyer's agent where your interests, not the seller's interests, are of paramount importance.

Having your own agent has the following advantages:

- Your time is not wasted by agents showing you unsuitable property to impress owners with the agents' activity or who want to push their own listings, which will mean more dollars for the agent rather than working for what is best for you.

- Your agent will work with you so that you are prequalified for a loan and know purchase limits.

- You are not going to be limited to properties listed for sale by agents. You will be exposed to properties that may be in probate or foreclosure, properties owned by lenders, and even properties for sale by owners.

- Your agent will analyze properties based on your needs and provide value estimates based on the market.

- Your agent will recommend properties to be considered and what should be offered and prepare the offer with your interests in mind.

- Your own agent will make certain you fully understand all aspects of a purchase contract before it is signed.

- Negative aspects of a property will be evaluated, and your agent will make certain that your offer is subject to a professional property inspection.

- Your agent will recommend the type of loan that best meets your needs and will work with you in locating the most advantageous loan terms.

- Your agent will be in contact with the lender, the seller, and the closing agent to avoid any problems during the closing process.

(1)

---

(2)

What Does It Cost to Have Your Own Agent?

In most cases, the fee paid to your agent will be entirely paid by the seller rather than taken from your pocket.

We are proud to be buyer's agents. To find out more about us and buyer representation, check our Web site, [www.urhome.com].

[UR Home Realty]

[1102 Bigelow Street]

[602-555-8200]

[agent@urhome.com]

Note: This flyer can be given to persons inquiring about properties and used as a mailing attachment.

Fixer-Upper Opportunity

UR
H O M E   R E A L T Y

_____ ← Date and address

_____
_____
_____

Dear _____ :

If you are one of the few people who can look beyond the [neglect and dirt] and visualize how this [3-bedroom, 2½-bath Cape Cod] can be reborn to model-home perfection, then a great opportunity can be yours.

View the details and photos [no. 49 on www.urhome.com] and contact me immediately.

Sincerely,

_____

Note: Never present a home as being dirty or neglected without the owner's permission.
If you send this as an e-mail and it is unsolicited, include your physical address as well as an opt-out mechanism such as the following:
☐ Please do not send me any further e-mails about real estate opportunities.

LAND, BUSINESS, AND INVESTMENT BUYER SOLICITATION

If you send an unsolicited e-mail, include your physical address as well as an opt-out mechanism such as the following:

☐ Please do not send me any further e-mails about real estate opportunities.

Builder Solicitation—Lots

UR
HOME REALTY

_____ ← Date and address

_____
_____
_____

Dear _____:

We have recently listed [20] lots in [Midvale Heights]. The lots all have [sewer and water installed and paid for], and they are competitively priced from [$67,500 to $92,500, with interesting terms possible].

I will be calling you in the next few days to discuss a convenient time to show you these desirable building sites.

Yours truly,

_____

Enclosure: ← Card

Note: The letter takes for granted the reader's interest, and the mention of a phone call forces the reader to spend a few seconds on the idea of lots in the area specified. The phone call should offer the choice of time of showing, not ask whether the builder wants a showing.

The do-not-call registry does not apply to business calls made to nonresidential numbers.

Adjoining-Owner Solicitation

UR
H O M E   R E A L T Y

_____ ← Date and address

_____
_____
_____

Dear _____:

I have just listed the property at [111 Midvale Lane] for sale. Because this property adjoins your property, we felt that you should have the first opportunity to purchase it before we advertise to the general public.

I am certain that you understand the advantage of owning this adjoining parcel. I will contact you in the next few days to provide any specific information you might desire.

Yours truly,

_____

Enclosure: ← Card

Note: This letter is a teaser. It creates urgency and a desire to know the price. This approach can be used for raw land, lots, farms, and even income or investment property. A great many properties are sold to adjoining property owners.

Owner of Similar Investment Property in Area

UR

HOME REALTY

_____ ← Date and address

_____
_____
_____

Dear _____:

When we listed the [24-unit apartment building at 3305–3307 Chestnut Boulevard], I immediately thought that this would be the ideal investment for the owner of the property at [3309 Chestnut Boulevard].

Because the property is [1. right next door to your property 2. so close to your property and is so similar], the management advantages of dual ownership are apparent.

The property is available at [1. an attractive price with flexible terms 2. $1.5 million with approximately ($150,000) down 3. a price and terms that will allow an immediate positive cash flow]. I will contact you in the next few days to discuss the advantages that this fine property can offer you.

Yours truly,

_____

P.S. If you are not interested in purchasing this property, perhaps you would consider selling your property. The advantages to a buyer owning both investment properties could make for an exceptional sale opportunity.

Enclosure: ← Card

Note: The P.S. raises the point that if the readers aren't buyers, they should be sellers. It also reinforces the advantages of owning two similar properties.

Commercial Tenant Solicitation of Ownership

UR
H O M E   R E A L T Y

_____ ← Date and address

_____
_____
_____

Dear [Ms. Perkins]:

How would you like your office to be in [1. Perkins Plaza   2. the Perkins Building] and not have to move?

Your present [1. office   2. commercial] building has just been placed on the market. It offers you a rare opportunity. You can be your own landlord and be entitled to income, any appreciation, and the tax benefits of depreciation instead of just a growing pile of rent receipts.

I will contact you in the next few days to show you how [Perkins Plaza] can become a reality.

Yours truly,

_____

Enclosure: ← Card, photo

Note: This letter should be sent to professional tenants and strong retail tenants. It has an excellent approach to pride by naming the building after the solicited buyer. Use your computer to put the tenant's name and/or logo on a digital photo of the building.

Tenant Solicitation—Office Condominium

UR
H O M E   R E A L T Y

_____ ← Date and address

_____
_____
_____

Dear _____:

Do you realize that you could move your office [less than three blocks] away and enjoy these advantages?

- ■ Absolute protection against future rent increases

- ■ The tax advantage of depreciation

- ■ Payments that increase your equity rather than worthless rent receipts

- ■ An investment that may show exceptional appreciation

- ■ A hedge against inflation

I have [1. several 2. an] outstanding office condominium[s] for sale that offer[s] you advantages that a rental cannot provide, and [1. is 2. are] bound to please your accountant. I should be able to make you an owner with little or no increase in actual monthly costs and a down payment tailored to your needs.

This may sound too good to be true, but I will prove it to you and your accountant. You can avoid saying "I should have . . . " in the future by investigating now.

I will be calling you to give you more information on this very special opportunity.

Yours truly,

_____

Enclosure: ← Card

Note: By canvassing the buildings close to your listing or by using a reverse directory, you can put together a sizable mailing list.
The do-not-call registry does not apply to nonresidential phone calls.

Franchisor—General Needs

To:

From: agent@urhome.com

Subject: Your Real Estate Needs

Attention: Real Estate Officer

I would like to be your real estate eyes and ears in [Clark and Humboldt Counties].

If you let me know your real estate needs regarding size, traffic count, access, demographics, price, rent, and so on, I would be happy to put my knowledge of the area to work for you.

Yours truly,

_____

111 Main Street
Podunk, CA 61405

☐ I do not wish to receive any future e-mails.

Note: Names and addresses of franchises are readily available from the Internet. One site to consider for names and addresses is *www.bison1.com/franchisepass.html.* An e-mail approach should be considered. An unsolicited solicitation must include your physical address and have an opt-out mechanism.

Franchisor—Specific Location

To:

From: agent@urhome.com

Subject: Excellent Franchise Location

Dear _____:

Our office has recently listed [a property at (55 Chestnut Boulevard)]. Click here for specific property information. Because of [access and traffic], I feel that it would be an excellent location for one of your franchises. An attractive [1. purchase price 2. lease] is available. Please let me know if you are interested.

I am willing to work with you in meeting your real estate needs in [Dade County]. If you let me know your specific interests, my eyes, ears, and expertise are available for you.

Yours truly,

_____

111 Main Street
Podunk, CA 61405

☐ I do not wish to receive any future e-mails.

Note: See the note on the previous e-mail.

White Elephant Investment

UR
HOME REALTY

_____ ← Date and address

_____
_____
_____

Dear _____:

Do you know

What to Do with a White Elephant?

We are looking for an investor with vision who can create a productive use for [a seven-story, 74,000-square-foot former textile plant with rail siding on a six-acre site north of Highway 30].

Although it's a problem, the price of [$890,000] reflects that. If you have a solution, someone else's problem can be your opportunity.

I will contact you in the next few days to arrange a private showing, and perhaps we can brainstorm a solution to the problem.

Yours truly,

_____

Enclosure: ← Card

Note: This is an excellent letter for owners of property in the area, creative investors, and developers. A letter such as this intrigues investors and speculators. It presents a puzzle to be solved and is an excellent way to gain initial personal access to major buyers of investment property. It can also be an effective e-mail to investors you have worked with in the past.

Safe Investment—Net Lease

UR
HOME REALTY

_____ ← Date and address

_____
_____
_____

Dear _____:

Do you want

Monotonous Income?

Would you like rent checks, month after month, year after year, while the tenant pays the taxes and makes the repairs? Would you like an investment that requires no decision making on your part?

Would you like to take full advantage of the tax code and shelter spendable dollars from taxation and pay taxes on your gains at a sharply reduced rate?

If a hands-off, tax friendly investment guaranteed by a financially strong tenant interests you and you can handle a [$250,000] down payment, then this could be the investment you have been waiting for.

I will be contacting you in the next few days, if you don't call me first, to arrange a private showing of a very special opportunity.

Yours truly,

_____

Enclosure: ← Card

Note: As written, this solicitation is for a triple-net property leased to a strong tenant. Mailings should be to investors owning larger quality properties as well as high-income individuals such as doctors, attorneys, and certified public accountants (CPAs). A letter such as this allows you to expand the size and quality of your list of potential real estate investors. Call recipients at their business rather than their residence to avoid do-not-call registry restrictions.

$1,000,000 Investment

UR
H O M E   R E A L T Y

_____ ← Date and address

_____
_____
_____

Dear _____ :

Want something

Better than a Money Market Account?

If a [million-dollar] price doesn't frighten you, I have a real estate investment that offers the following:

- [A long-term lease]
- [A financially strong tenant]
- A hedge against inflation
- Great leverage opportunities
- Tax-sheltered income
- Likely appreciation
- [Professional management]

I will call you in the next few days to discuss the benefits offered by this extraordinary real estate investment.

Yours truly,

_____

Enclosure: ← Card

Note: Income will be sheltered by depreciation. The do-not-call registry regulations apply to residential calls but not to business phones.

Flipper Opportunity

To:

From: agent@urhome.com

Subject: Flipper Opportunity

Attachment(s):   Profit Opportunity

Dear _____:

Be the first to check out this [3-bedroom, 2-bath Mid-Century Modern] in desirable [West Village].

Combine your imagination with some hard work and the result could be exceptional profit. [1. View the details and photos (no. 47 on www.urhome.com) and contact me immediately.] [2. Click on the attachment to view opportunity.]

Sincerely,

_____

Note: Use e-mails to persons who visited fixer-upper open houses or expressed an interest in fixer-uppers, as well as profit opportunities. If you do not have permission to send property information, you must include your physical address and an opt-out sentence. [□ Please do not send me any further e-mails about real estate opportunities.]

Profit Opportunity

To:

From: agent@urhome.com

Subject: Profit Opportunity for a Real Estate Investor

Dear _____:

Last month our office sold a [house] for [$390,000]. An investor purchased the house through our office [three months ago] for [$270,000]. This made for a very happy investor.

I have just obtained [1. a similar listing, which   2. an exceptional listing, which because of unusual circumstances] can be purchased for [$312,000].

If you are interested in a profit opportunity, contact me now because this opportunity is going to be snapped up by a very fortunate investor.

Sincerely,

_____

Note: If you do not have permission to send property information, a physical address and an opt-out sentence must be included:
[□ Please do not send me any further e-mails as to real estate opportunities.]
Make certain the owner knows you will be marketing to investors who wish to resell for a profit.

Referral Investor

UR
H O M E   R E A L T Y

_____ ← Date and address

_____
_____
_____

Dear _____:

[Alice Smith] recommended that I contact you. We have [1. just listed 2. available] an exceptional investment opportunity that [she] thought might interest you.

It is a [low-risk] property offering the [possibility of extraordinary appreciation coupled with tax-sheltered income]. It would require a down payment of about [$110,000].

[1. I will be contacting you 2. Call me today if you would like] to determine whether this property would fulfill your investment needs.

Yours truly,

_____

Enclosure: ← Card

Note: This letter gives little detail other than amount of down payment. It is intended to get the recipients to consider owning investment property and to prepare them so you can qualify them according to their specific needs. Although you must have an actual property, the letter is used to tantalize. Providing more details would increase the likelihood that the recipient will interpret some of those details as negative. Again, be aware of the do-not-call registry regulations.

Syndicate Formation

UR
HOME REALTY

_____ ← Date and address

_____
_____
_____

Dear _____:

I am putting together a small group of local investors [1. to take part in an exceptional investment opportunity as limited partners 2. to take advantage of the exceptional opportunities available now in distressed income property].

[1. (Joe Jones) has recommended you as a person who would appreciate taking part in this opportunity. 2. You indicated some time ago that I should contact you if a really great opportunity presented itself.]

Because you are knowledgeable in investment matters, you will understand the desirability of prime [low-risk] real estate investments [at a bargain basement price].

Investors must be able to make a [$100,000] minimum investment. [1. I will call you to determine your interest in 2. Please call me at (602-555-8200) if you are interested in] attending an informal meeting of potential investors at [my home at 1744 Midvale Lane] on [Saturday morning, April 10, at 10:00 AM]. [After I have discussed the opportunity and answered any questions, those who are interested will have an opportunity to visit the property.]

Yours truly,

_____

Enclosure: ← Card

Note: A morning home meeting provides a nonthreatening atmosphere. Also, a group meeting tends to reduce apprehension. For a syndicate solicitation, be certain that you have checked your state laws. Syndicates may be subject to federal and state registration unless they fit into an exemption. Consult an attorney before you attempt to form a syndicate. Calls should be to business phones, or the do-not-call registry will have to be consulted.

Notice to Business Owner of Related Business for Sale

UR

H O M E   R E A L T Y

_____ ← Date and address

_____
_____
_____

Dear _____:

Because you are in the [retail hardware] business, you now have an exceptional opportunity for expansion.

We have just listed for sale a [successful hardware store] that offers great potential. The books are open to you and your accountant. I will be calling you with more details. I believe that this opportunity deserves your immediate attention.

Yours truly,

_____

Enclosure: ← Card

Note: This letter is a teaser to excite interest. The letter should give very little information about the business and not identify the particular business being offered at this time.

Keep in mind that financial information concerning a property or business should never be given to anyone without the owner's permission.

Supplier or Wholesaler—Business Opportunity

UR

H O M E   R E A L T Y

_____ ← Date and address

_____
_____
_____

Dear _____ :

Because you are a [plumbing] [1. distributor   2. wholesaler], I thought that you should be aware of the [plumbing supply business] we recently listed for sale. [Jones Plumbing Supplies] is located at [105 Midvale], and the price of [$250,000] includes [all fixtures, vehicles, and an advantageous lease]. The books are open to a qualified buyer [and owner financing is possible].

I will call you in the next few days to ask for your help in identifying any of your customers who might be interested in an exceptional expansion opportunity.

Yours truly,

_____

Enclosure: ← Card

Note: Suppliers have a stake in finding a buyer because a happy buyer will feel indebted to the supplier. Many businesses are sold to buyers based on information gained from suppliers.

For a supplier letter, the business should be identified, and a price or price range should be indicated.

Operating Income and Expenses

UR
HOME REALTY

FAX   Date: _____

To: _____   Attn: _____

From: _____   Pages w/cover: _____

Dear _____:

The following is a statement of income and expenses for the property located at [19 Partridge Lane] [as requested]. The figures set forth are based on [1. a copy of the latest tax return provided by the owner 2. a statement provided by the owner 3. the books provided to us by the owner 4. the property management statements 5. information furnished by the owner's accountant].

Income

Scheduled gross annual income	$ _____
Vacancy and collection loss	($ _____)
Adjusted gross annual income	$ _____

Expenses

Taxes [2011]	$ _____
Insurance cost [2011]	$ _____
Policy provider [Jones Underwriters]	
Utilities [2011]	$ _____
Management costs [2011]	$ _____
Maintenance and repairs [2011]	$ _____
Total expenses	($ _____)
[(before debt service)]	
Net operating income	$ _____
[(not considering debt service)]	

(1)

(2)

It should be pointed out that just a [3] percent annual increase in rents would increase the net income by [over $50,000] within [six] years, and rentals in the area are currently experiencing an annual increase of [over 3] percent a year. I will be calling you to answer any questions you may have and to show you why I feel this investment opportunity deserves your immediate and serious consideration.

Yours truly,

_____

Enclosure: ← Card

Note: Minor modification would turn this letter into an operating income and expense statement to be attached to property briefs (flyers describing properties). This information could be provided by e-mail. You must have an owner's permission to give out income and expense data.

SERVICING THE LISTING

Time is generally not a critical factor in letters to owners regarding servicing the listing unless they deal with a purchase offer; however, some parties prefer e-mails. Where time is important, it is best to call or e-mail individuals.

Thank You for Listing

UR

H O M E   R E A L T Y

_____ ← Date and address

_____
_____
_____

Dear _____:

As the broker with [UR Home Realty], I appreciate the confidence you have shown by making [UR Home Realty] your exclusive agent for the sale of your home.

I want you to know that you can expect us to be diligent and professional in our efforts to make a favorable sale on your [home]. We have already [1. prepared initial advertising 2. placed initial advertising 3. included a virtual tour of your home on our Web site (www.urhome.com) 4. Placed photographs and details of your home on (four) additional Web sites] and, of course, provided information on your home to [our multiple listing service]. We will keep you up to date on our progress.

[Lynn Smith] of our office will be working with you throughout the sales process and even after the sale to ensure a satisfactory closing. If you have any questions concerning your property or our efforts, please contact [Mr. Smith].

I look forward to presenting you with a buyer.

Yours truly,

_____

Enclosure: ← Card, [hard copy of web postings]

Note: For a thank you, a letter rather than an e-mail is preferred.

Thank You for Listing—Out-of-Town Owner

UR

HOME REALTY

_____ ← Date and address

_____
_____
_____

Dear _____:

I would like to thank you for showing your confidence in [UR Home Realty] by appointing us your exclusive agent for the sale of your property. We have already entered your [home] on [www.urhome.com] [as well as (3) additional Web sites.] Information about your home is now available to millions of home hunters on a global basis. Locally, the [Westhaven Board of REALTORS®] has [712] agents in [57] offices who want to sell your home.

Because you live a great distance from our office, would you please provide us with the following information?

1. The name and phone number of a local person to contact in the event of an emergency _____

2. The name and address of your property insurance agent and policy number
   _____

3. The name and phone number of your local attorney (if applicable)
   _____

4. The name and phone number of the following, as applicable:

■ Gardening services _____

■ Pool service _____

■ Protection service _____

■ Pest control service _____

■ Cleaning and maintenance service _____

■ Homeowners' association _____

(1)

(2)

5.   Your cell phone number _____

6.   Your e-mail address _____

7.   Your fax number (if applicable) _____

You should contact your insurance agent to make certain that you are maintaining adequate coverage.

I look forward to telling you that your [home] has been sold.

Sincerely,

_____

Enclosure: ← Card, [hard copies of web postings.]

Neighborhood Information Request

UR
_____
H O M E   R E A L T Y

_____ ← Date and address

_____
_____
_____

Dear _____:

Having an in-depth knowledge of your neighborhood and neighbors can give us a competitive edge over less-informed sales agents who represent other properties.

We value your knowledge of your community and would therefore appreciate your sharing this knowledge by completing this form to the best of your ability to help us sell your home.

1. Neighborhood features you feel a buyer would be most pleased with:
   _____
   _____

2. School districts: _____

3. School-bus stops: _____

4. Names, ages, and schools attended by neighborhood children (include private schools):

   _____   _____   _____
   _____   _____   _____
   _____   _____   _____
   _____   _____   _____
   _____   _____   _____

5. Youth activities in the area (Little League, junior hockey, soccer league, etc.):
   _____

6. Public recreational facilities in the area (parks, pools, playgrounds, tennis courts, etc.): _____

7. Nearest public transportation route: _____

(1)

---

(2)

8. Nearest medical facility: _____

9. Nearest community center (for children, seniors, etc.): _____
    _____

10. Nearest houses of worship: _____

11. Nearest shopping area: _____

12. General information on closest neighbors: _____
    _____

13. The professions of people living in the area who might interest a possible
    buyer (doctor, banker, attorney, professor, or celebrity): _____
    _____

14. Describe the interests of the person or family you feel would best appreciate
    your home and neighborhood: _____
    _____

15. Other information that would be of interest to a likely buyer: _____
    _____
    _____

Please send your completed form to my attention in the enclosed postage-paid
envelope.

We greatly appreciate your help in providing this information about your neighborhood.

Appreciatively yours,

_____

Enclosure: ← Card

Note: This letter not only gains you sales ammunition but also shows the owner that
you appreciate the neighborhood and neighbors and are making your best efforts on
their behalf.
Include a self-addressed stamped envelope.

Instruction Sheet Transmittal

UR
H O M E   R E A L T Y

_____ ← Date and address

_____
_____
_____

Dear _____:

In marketing your home, we are competing against [1. dozens 2. hundreds] of other owners who are all after the same pool of buyers. To compete successfully, we want to gain every possible advantage. The enclosed instruction sheet allows you to play an important role in obtaining the best possible sale for your home.

Please call me if you have any questions.

Thanking you in advance for your cooperation,

_____

Enclosure: ← Card, homeowner instructions

Homeowner Instructions

Homeowner Hints for a Successful Sale

I. Exterior

    A. Grass and shrubs. Keep trimmed. Consider a fast-greening fertilizer such as ammonium sulfate (inexpensive) for a deep green lawn.

    B. Pets. If you have a dog, clean up any dog dirt on a daily basis. If you have a cat, change the litter box daily. Pets should be restrained or kept away from the property during showings.

    C. Fences. Make any needed repairs. A neat, well-painted fence gives a positive impression.

    D. Flowers. Plant seasonal, blooming flowers, especially near the front door and in patio areas. A profusion of color can have your home half-sold before the door is even opened.

    E. Bird feeders. Hummingbird feeders and bird houses create a pleasant mood, especially when they are close to any patio area.

    F. Paint. Concentrating on the following two areas may be the most profitable:

        ■ **Front door.** Front door should be refinished or painted if it shows excessive wear.

        ■ **Condition of exterior paint.** Often only the trim or, depending on sun exposure, only one or two sides of the house need painting. Keep in mind that paint is cheap compared to the extra dollars a home with a clean, fresh appearance will bring.

    G. Lawn furniture. Place lawn furniture and barbeque in an attractive, leisure arrangement. A badminton net or croquet setup also gives a positive image.

    H. Roof. If the roof needs to be repaired or replaced, it's best to have the work done. Otherwise, buyers will want to deduct the cost even if your price already reflects the required work. Delaying repairs can actually cost you twice as much.

(1)

(2)

II. Interior

A. Housekeeping. Because you are competing against model homes, your home must look as much like a model as possible. Floors, bath fixtures, and appliances must be sparkling. Consider using a car wax on appliances. Make beds early in the day. Unmade beds and late sleepers create a negative image.

B. Odors and aromas. Avoid heavy frying, using vinegar, or cooking strong-smelling foods. Odors often last and work against the image you are trying to create. On the other hand, some smells have a positive effect on people: Baked bread, apple pie, chocolate cookies, and cinnamon rolls are examples of foods that can help sell your home. Consider keeping packaged cookie or bread dough in the refrigerator. Just before a scheduled showing, the smell of these baking foods can be a great help to us. If you or your family members smoke, don't smoke in your home and don't allow guests to smoke. Stale tobacco odors can be masked with some odor sprays. If the temperature allows it, open windows and air out the house every morning.

C. Paint. If you have leftover paint, you can accomplish a great deal by doing touch-ups where needed. If the surface is dark, repaint with light colors such as off-white, oyster, light beige, or pale yellow. Light colors make rooms appear fresh as well as larger.

D. Plumbing. Repair leaky faucets. Make certain that you don't have a gurgling toilet. Replace cracked or stained toilet seats.

E. Shades and blinds. Replace torn shades or broken blinds.

F. Drapes. If drapes need cleaning, have it done. If they are old and worn, stained or dark, consider replacing them with either light-colored drapes or off-white vinyl vertical blinds. (Large discount and home improvement centers usually carry standard sizes at reasonable prices.)

G. Carpets. Dirty carpets should be either professionally steam-cleaned (preferred), or you should rent a heavy-duty cleaner. If the carpet is badly worn, replace it with new carpet (and a quality pad) in a neutral color. Consider either a plush or a Berber carpet.

H. Lighting. If any room appears dark, increase the wattage of the light bulbs. Before a showing, open the blinds and drapes and turn on the lights, even during the day—you want the house as bright as possible. Be sure that your light fixtures and windows are clean.

I. Closets. If closets appear crowded, remove unneeded items and put them in boxes. They can be stacked neatly in a corner of the basement, attic, or garage.

ı

---

(3)

J. **Too much furniture.** Many homes appear crowded, with too many pieces of large furniture. Consider putting excess furniture in a storage locker.

K. **Clutter.** Remove knickknacks and photographs. Remove all items from the refrigerator door. Clear kitchen countertops of small appliances.

L. **Garage and basement.** Spruce up your work area. Consider a garage sale to get rid of items you no longer need. Put excess items in boxes and stack them neatly in a corner. Consider using a commercial garage floor cleaner on oil and grease marks on the garage floor and driveway. You might consider a commercial steam cleaner (not a carpet cleaner).

M. **Temperature.** On cold days, a natural fire in the fireplace will help us sell your home. Start the fire before the showing is scheduled. On hot days, consider turning the air conditioner four to five degrees cooler than normal. The contrast will seem phenomenal, making a very positive impression. In moderate weather, open windows for fresh air.

N. **Valuables.** Store small valuables in a safe place.

III. Your Best Role during Showings

A. When your home is shown, it's best that you disappear. Buyers feel restrained with an owner present. If buyers hesitate to voice their concerns, then their questions cannot be answered and their problems cannot be solved.

B. If you must remain, try to stay in one area. Excellent places to be are working in the garden, on the lawn, or in the workshop. These activities create a positive image. While soft music is fine, turn off the TV.

C. Never, never follow the agent around the house during the showing, volunteer any information, or answer questions the buyers ask the agent. You have engaged professional real estate salespeople. We will ask you questions if necessary.

[UR Home Realty]

[602-555-8200]

Note: Besides using these instructions as an enclosure with a letter, you can also use them as part of your listing presentation or as a handout after listing.

Marketing Plan for Home

UR
H O M E   R E A L T Y

_____ ← Date and address

_____
_____
_____

Dear _____:

I would like to share with you our marketing plan for your home.

- Install a sign [and talking sign].

- Take photographs of your home.

- Give you suggestions to help increase the marketability of your home.

- Prepare a property brief (descriptive sheet) with a photo of your home emphasizing the desirable characteristics of the property.

- Place [1. photo 2. virtual tour] of your home, along with detailed information, on our office Web site [www.urhome.com], as well as at least [three] other Web sites covering local, regional, and national properties.

- Install a lockbox on the property to aid in showing your home to prospective buyers when you are not available.

- Send property briefs to other agents active in the area and discuss with them the benefits your home has to offer.

- Leave a supply of property briefs at your home for open house visitors and agent showings.

- Prepare a minimum of three separate classified ads for your home.

- Schedule ad placement.

- Meet with you to show you how you can help in the marketing of your home.

- Prepare for and conduct [our office agent visitation and] board visitation by real estate agents.

- Discuss your home with agents who toured your home to find ways to enhance its marketability.

(1)

---

(2)

- ▦ Our agents will call or e-mail all likely prospects they are currently working with about your home.

- ▦ Send direct mailings to area neighbors to enlist help in selecting a new neighbor.

- ▦ Prepare for and conduct an open house.

- ▦ Follow up on all leads generated by calls about or visits to your home.

- ▦ Make weekly calls to all agents who used the lockbox about the interest of their buyers.

- ▦ Communicate [weekly] with you on our efforts and progress with your home as well as changes in the area market.

- ▦ Advertise your home along with other homes in your area and in the same price range, as well as continue our program of institutional advertising.

Continue to make our best efforts to locate a buyer as well as internally evaluate those efforts until we are successful.

If you have any questions about this marketing plan outline, please call me.

Yours truly,

_____

Enclosure: ← Card

Note: You could use this as an attachment to a letter to an owner expressing thanks for the listing, as well as a tool to obtain listings.

Seller's Net Proceeds Estimate Transmittal

UR
H O M E   R E A L T Y

_____ ← Date and address

_____
_____
_____

Dear _____:

Enclosed is a seller's net proceeds worksheet I have prepared for your property at [41 Greer Street].

The net reflects [your present mortgage being paid off and a sale at the list price of ($239,000)].

I believe the figures on the worksheet are reliable, but they are estimates only and are not guaranteed.

If you have any questions, please call me.

Yours truly,

_____

Enclosure: ← Card

Note: Ordinarily the seller's net information should be given to the owner at the time the listing is taken.

Seller's Net Proceeds Estimate Worksheet

UR

H O M E   R E A L T Y

Estimated Seller's Net

[Seller]

Credits

Sale price	$_____
Impound account balance	$_____
Prepaid insurance	$_____
Prepaid taxes	$_____
Other credits	$_____
Total credits	$_____

[Property Address]

Debits

Loans	$_____
Other encumbrances	$_____
Loan prepayment penalties	$_____
Agent fees	$_____
Escrow/attorney	$_____
Abstract/title insurance	$_____
Transfer tax	$_____
Termite inspection	$_____
Real estate taxes	$_____
Unpaid assessments	$_____
Home protection plan	$_____
Other	$_____
Total debits	$_____
Total credits	$_____
Total debits	– $_____
Seller net	$_____

Note: Seller net would be cash and/or carryback financing in which the seller is financing the buyer.

Agent Property Evaluation Transmittal Letter

UR
HOME REALTY

_____← Date and address

_____
_____
_____

Dear _____:

Enclosed are copies of agent property evaluations made by agents at our [1. office caravan (and the) 2. multiple listing service caravan] on [October 14]. The evaluations can provide valuable information about your home.

I will be contacting you in the next few days to discuss these evaluations.

Yours truly,

_____

Enclosure: ← Card, agent property evaluations

Agent Property Evaluation

UR
H O M E   R E A L T Y

Property address: _____ Date: _____

Name of owner(s): _____

   1. Feature of the home that will be most appealing to buyer:

      _____

      _____

      _____

      _____

   2. Features or lack of features that buyers are likely to view as a negative:

      _____

      _____

      _____

      _____

   3. I feel that the price is   ☐ too high ☐ too low ☐ realistic

      By how much? $ _____ Why? _____

      _____

      _____

   4. To increase salability, the owner should consider the following:

      _____

      _____

      _____

      _____

_____

Evaluator

Note: Give this form to agents who view the home at office or MLS caravans, as well as those who attend an agent open house. You would fill in the property address and name of owner. Give the completed forms to the owner.

Web Site Information Transmittal

UR
H O M E   R E A L T Y

_____ ← Date and address

_____
_____
_____

Dear _____:

Enclosed is a printout of the information about your home that we have posted on our Web site, [www.urhome.com]. Features of the Web site include the ability [1. to view several photos of your home 2. to enlarge photos 3. for a viewer to have a virtual tour of your home, moving from room to room as in a physical viewing].

We have also posted the Web site material to the following additional Web sites: [www.PalmSpringsHomes.com, www.CARealtor.com, www.SuCasa.net, and www. Realtor.com].

As the world becomes technology-oriented, the Internet has increased in value as a marketing tool. However, this is just one of many marketing tools we will employ to sell your home. You will see other methods in your [weekly] progress reports.

Looking forward to a successful sale,

_____

` Enclosure: ← Card, Web site printout of Web site entry

Ad Copy Transmittal

UR
H O M E   R E A L T Y

_____ ← Date and address

_____
_____
_____

Dear _____:

Enclosed is a copy of a classified advertisement that appeared in the [Riverside Enterprise] on [June 14 and 15].

I am certain that you realize that we receive many inquiries from our institutional advertising, as well as from ads for specific property, and that we follow up on every inquiry. Because we track every call, we even know who called after business hours and failed to leave a message.

What you may not be aware of is that relatively few buyers actually end up purchasing the home they originally inquired about. After qualifying a buyer's needs and financial standing, we frequently find that the property in question does not fit the particular buyer. The buyer is then shown a number of other properties. In this way, every ad we place within a general price range serves as a sales tool for every home we have within that price range.

We will use our best efforts to promote the sale of your home. All our advertisements benefit you, even those not specifically for your property. We have proven that our advertising methods work, and I feel confident they will be successful for your home.

Yours truly,

_____

Enclosure: ← Card, ad copy

Progress Report

UR
H O M E   R E A L T Y

_____ ← Date and address

_____
_____
_____

Dear _____:

This note is to keep you informed of our efforts on your behalf. During the [week] of [September 4–10], we have done the following:

■ Advertised your home in [two newspapers] using [three] ads with insertions on [5] days. [This is in addition to our institutional advertising and ads for other property in the same price range.]

■ Answered [16] inquiries on your home and have had [four] showings by our own salespeople

■ Had [five] showings by salespeople from cooperating offices

■ Had [one] open house and registered [17] guests

■ Kept your home active in the Midvale Multiple-Listing Service Web site, which is available to [107] offices and more than [1,000] salespeople, as well as on [three] Web sites covering regional and national properties, plus our own site [www.ur-home.net]

■ Followed up on every lead received from a variety of sources

[Although we have not yet received an offer on your home,] we are very optimistic and will continue our efforts on your behalf.

Yours truly,

_____

Enclosure: ← Card

Weekly Progress Report (Form)

UR
HOME REALTY

_____ ← Date and address

_____
_____
_____

Dear _____ :

The following weekly progress report describes our marketing efforts for your [home]:

- [Week ending]: [7 August]
- Property: [3961 Hampton Lane]
- Owners: [J.C. and April Clark]
- Number of phone inquiries: [13]
- Number of showings by our office: [3]
- Advertising: [2 ads in Daily Sentinel as well as feature in Home Showcase and 4 Web sites]
- Electronic lockbox activity: [5 showings by other offices]
- Open House
  - Date(s): [5 August]
  - Number of visitors: [8]

Comments of other agents and prospective buyers: [Great neighborhood and lovely patio. Carpeting will have to be replaced by buyer, and kitchen could use new countertop. One prospect indicated that the wallpaper was dated and should be removed.]

If you have any questions, please contact me.

Yours truly,

_____

Enclosure: ← Card

Note: Some office management systems prepare progress reports.

Open House Results

UR
H O M E   R E A L T Y

_____ ← Date and address

_____
_____
_____

Dear _____:

This is just a short note to let you know about the open house for your home on [December 12].

We advertised the open house on [December 11 and 12] in [both the Daily News and the Westside Sentinel] and set up [directional signs, open house signs, and flags]. [We also sent letters and e-mails to (neighbors) and (visitors to other open houses).]

I registered [14] visitors to the open house. [1. Several additional visitors declined to register. 2. I was encouraged by favorable comments from a number of the visitors.]

I will be contacting all the visitors to the open house within the next few days to ascertain their needs as well as their interest in your home.

[The market is relatively slow right now; therefore, I think we need to reexamine our strategy to excite buyers. I will call you in the next few days to discuss ways in which we can increase the desirability of your home.]

[I am very hopeful that, with our continued efforts, we will be able to find that special buyer for your home.]

Yours truly,

_____

Enclosure: ← Card

Change of Agents

UR

HOME REALTY

_____ ⟵ Date and address

_____
_____
_____

Dear _____:

[Keith Swift] of our office will be taking over the primary responsibility of the sale of your home from [Karen Jones], who is no longer with our office. [Mr. Swift] will call you in the next few days to discuss our past and future efforts on your behalf.

If you have any questions at all, please do not hesitate to contact either [Mr. Swift] or me. I have enclosed one of [Mr. Swift's] cards.

Yours truly,

_____

Enclosure: ⟵ New agent's card

Note: A better approach would be for new agents to call the owners and arrange to meet with them to personally tell them they will be working with them on the sale of their home.

Price Adjustment Request—Out-of-Area Owner
New Comparative Market Analysis

UR
H O M E   R E A L T Y

_____ ← Date and address

_____
_____
_____

Dear _____:

Because of changes in the real estate marketplace, we have updated and enclosed a comparative market analysis indicating the current value of your home.

From the sales figures of comparable homes recently sold, as well as from the asking prices of similar homes that remain unsold, you will see that homes priced above the present market value are not selling. You will also see the necessity for a price adjustment to conform to market conditions. The marketplace ultimately determines at what price a property will sell.

I have enclosed a [1. new listing 2. listing addendum] reflecting the current real estate market. Please sign and return [three] copies to our office.

I will be calling you in the next few days to answer any questions that you might have.

Yours truly,

_____

Enclosure: ← Card, comparative market analysis, listing addendum, self-addressed stamped envelope

---

Note: It is better to blame the market rather than the home or the agency for the fact that a property has not sold. Never suggest "lowering" a price—the price is "adjusted" to reflect the market. Generally, a request to adjust a listing price should be made in person rather than by letter.

Price Adjustment Request—New Listing at Lower Price

UR
H O M E   R E A L T Y

_____ ← Date and address

_____
_____
_____

Dear _____:

Several homes in your area have recently come on the market.

Address	Size	Age	Price
[11 LaMont Circle]	[2,800 sq ft]	[4 Years]	[$465,000]
[74826 Crestview]	[2,650 sq ft]	[1 Year]	[$449,500]
[524 Adrian Way]	[2,790 sq ft]	[7 Years]	[$458,000]

[1. Listing information 2. A descriptive flyer] for each home is included.

You will note that [two] of the listings are for [1. larger 2. newer] homes. In addition, [one of the homes has a pool]. All [three] homes are priced lower than the price we have set for your home. Because of its price, by comparison your home will now appear to a buyer as being overpriced.

The market appears to be softening, which reduces the likelihood of selling your home at the list price of [$490,000]. If your home is to compete successfully in this market, I strongly suggest that the price be adjusted to [$459,000]. I have included a listing addendum reflecting this adjustment. Please sign and return [three] copies to this office.

Yours truly,

_____

Enclosure: ← Card, property flyers, listing addendum, self-addressed stamped envelope

Note: This letter will make the owners realize that they are competing with other owners. It does not criticize the property; it places the blame on the market. Photos of the new listing can be shown by printing out the material from a Web site. Again, price adjustment requests should be made only by written communication when a face-to-face meeting is not possible.

Price Adjustment Request—Lender Appraisal Below List Price

UR
_____
H O M E   R E A L T Y

_____ ← Date and address

_____
_____
_____

Dear _____:

I have just received the enclosed appraisal by [Midvale Savings and Loan] on your home.

Although I may not fully agree with this appraisal, it will nevertheless significantly affect prospective buyers, who will be reluctant to buy at a price above their lender's appraisal.

I therefore believe that it is in your best interest to adjust the price to reflect this appraisal. I have enclosed an addendum reflecting the new price. Please sign and return [two] copies.

[I will be calling you to answer any questions that you might have.]

Yours truly,

_____

Enclosure: ← Card, appraisal report, listing addendum, self-addressed stamped envelope

Note: Never suggest "lowering" a price. The price is "adjusted" to reflect the lender's appraisal. Any request to adjust a listing price should be made in person whenever possible, rather than by letter.

Price Adjustment Request—Property Originally Priced Above Comparative Market Analysis

---

UR

H O M E   R E A L T Y

_____ ← Date and address

_____
_____
_____

Dear _____:

At the time we listed your home for sale at [111 Midvale Drive], our comparative market analysis indicated it had a market value of [$425,500]. Based on your decision as owner, the house was placed on the market at [$500,000].

Your home has now been on the market for [90] days. During this time, we have advertised the property, called prospective buyers to discuss it, [held an open house,] posted photos and property details [including a virtual tour] on [three] Web sites, as well as to our multiple listing service, which has [93] offices and [1,141] agents. Despite our best efforts, we have only shown your home to [seven] prospective buyers. [Several of those who have seen it expressed the opinion that your home, while desirable, is overpriced compared to other available properties.]

Therefore, in our professional judgment, the price should be adjusted to [$425,500], the figure that was indicated by our comparative market analysis. If you truly want to sell your home, I am certain that you will agree. I have enclosed a listing addendum that reflects this adjustment. Please sign and return [three] copies to my office.

I will be calling you to answer any questions that you might have.

Yours truly,

_____

Enclosure: ← Card, comparative market analysis, listing addendum, self-addressed stamped envelope

---

Note: See comments in the previous letters.

Price Adjustment Request—Raise Price Based on Market Competition

---

UR
HOME   REALTY

_____ ← Date and address

_____
_____
_____

Dear _____:

Recent sales indicate that [home] prices are escalating. We have therefore prepared a new comparative market analysis for your home at [1 1 1 Midvale Trail].

You'll see that it indicates that our current asking price is too low. While the low price would likely mean a very quick sale, we feel we can get you a higher price within a reasonable time.

I have included a [1. listing addendum   2. new listing] reflecting a price adjustment to [$450,000]. Please sign and return [three] copies to this office.

I will call you in a few days to answer any questions that you might have.

Yours truly,

_____

Enclosure: ← Card, comparative market analysis, listing addendum, self-ad-
                  dressed stamped envelope

Note: A letter is not the preferred method of asking for a price adjustment and should be used only when personal contact cannot be made.

Price Adjustment Request—Fixer-Upper

_____

UR
HOME REALTY

_____ ← Date and address

_____
_____
_____

Dear _____:

The condition of your home at [55 Lynn Court] has made a sale difficult in our market. As you know, [1. the house needs decorating 2. the carpets need replacing 3. the home generally is showing the effects of its age]. Unless you are willing to extensively rehabilitate the property, I would like your permission to advertise your home as a fixer-upper. This type of ad has strong appeal to many buyers who are not afraid of hard work and who meet these challenges with enthusiasm.

To attract this type of buyer, a price adjustment would be necessary. I suggest [1. a price of ($279,500) 2. we offer the purchaser a renovation and decorating adjustment of ($40,000)]. I have enclosed a listing addendum that reflects this adjustment. Please sign and return [three] copies to this office.

I am confident that taking this approach will mean a timely sale of your property. I will be contacting you in the next few days to answer any questions that you might have.

Yours truly,

_____

Enclosure: ← Card, listing addendum, self-addressed stamped envelope

_____

Note: Again, the preferred method of communicating a request for a price adjustment is personal contact. An owner might find a "decorating adjustment" more palatable than a "price adjustment."

Request for Minor Repairs

UR

H O M E   R E A L T Y

_____ ← Date and address

_____
_____
_____

Dear _____:

Several prospective buyers who have visited your home have commented about the [1. broken porch railing 2. broken window panes]. Although this is not a major problem, it nevertheless presents a significant negative image to prospective buyers. We feel that it would be in your best interest to arrange for the necessary repair as soon as possible.

If you are unable to make the repair[s] yourself, I would be happy to recommend a [1. handyman 2. contractor] with whom I have had good experience in the past.

I will be calling you to answer any questions that you might have.

Yours truly,

_____

Enclosure: ← Card

Request for Listing Extension

UR
_____
H O M E   R E A L T Y

_____ ← Date and address

_____
_____
_____

Dear _____:

The activity concerning your home has increased, and I feel certain we will be successful in arranging a sale. We have been making our utmost efforts on your behalf because we realize how important a sale is to you. During the last [six] months, we have placed numerous advertisements, placed photos of your home on [three] Web sites, held open houses, and provided information on your home to [our local real estate organization], which has [39] offices and [932] salespeople.

We want to not only continue our efforts but also increase them until we are successful. [1. To make our Web site listings stand out, we will be preparing a virtual tour of your home so prospective buyers can move from room to room, up and down, and left to right while viewing their computer. 2. We are scheduling open houses every week with greater newspaper coverage. 3. Your home will be featured as (Home of the Week) in the (Midvale Homebuyers Guide).]

I have enclosed an extension to our agency agreement. Please sign and return [three] copies so we can continue our efforts to consummate a sale without interruption. I will be contacting you in the next few days to answer any questions you might have and to discuss a marketing plan that will mean a successful sale.

Yours truly,

_____

Enclosure: ← Card, agency agreement extension, self-addressed stamped
                envelope

Note: Ideally, a request for a listing extension should be made in person. It is easier to say no to a letter than to a person. The words "agency agreement" are more positive than "listing." "Agency" implies a benefit while "listing" implies payment of a fee.

Listing Extended—Thank You

UR
H O M E   R E A L T Y

_____ ← Date and address

_____

_____

_____

Dear _____:

Thank you for the confidence you have shown in [UR Home Realty] in extending our agency agreement on your [home] at [27142 Lewis Lane].

I want you to know that we are dedicating our utmost efforts to the successful sale of your home. We realize how much a sale means to you. I feel certain that we will succeed in our quest for a buyer.

[Enclosed is an executed copy of the agency agreement extension.]

Yours truly,

_____

Enclosure: ← Card, [signed agency agreement extension]

Listing Expired—Thank You for Listing

UR
HOME REALTY

_____ ← Date and address

_____
_____
_____

Dear _____:

We regret that you have decided not to renew our agency agreement. However, I want to thank you for having given [UR Home Realty] the opportunity to serve as your sales agent.

[1. The market conditions were not favorable for a sale at the list price, although market conditions are now showing an improvement. 2. I feel a listing extension would result in a sale. However, with the present market, I suggest a listing range of ($400,000) to ($475,000).]

Should you decide that you wish to use the services of [UR Home Realty] again, I have enclosed a new agency agreement. By signing and returning [three] copies to our office, you will again be certain that we will use our best efforts to serve your interests. [The new agency agreement reflects our recommendations.]

[I will be calling you in the next few days to offer you some suggestions that should help in marketing your home.]

Yours truly,

_____

Enclosure: ← Card, agency agreement

Purchase Offer Transmittal #1

UR
H O M E   R E A L T Y

FAX   Date: _____

To: _____   Attn: _____

From: _____   Pages w/cover: _____

Dear _____:

It took a lot of effort, but we were successful in obtaining the enclosed offer on your [home]. I believe it to be a reasonable offer because it provides you with [93 percent] of the offering price.

If you agree with me, please sign the enclosed purchase offer where indicated and fax the accepted purchase offer to me immediately. The buyers are not legally bound to this purchase offer until a signed acceptance is received. Until that time, they have the right to cancel their offer without penalty.

Please call me at [800-760-2111] as soon as you receive this fax so I can explain the entire offer and answer any questions you might have.

Yours truly,

_____

Note: Showing the offer as a percentage of the offering price tends to minimize the difference. Using the term "offering price" reminds the owner that this price is not sacred but is merely a hoped-for price.

You create a sense of urgency by correctly pointing out that a buyer can back out before acceptance. Although sellers may refuse low offers, they don't like to allow the buyer to back out once an offer is made.

Whenever possible, offers should be presented in person. Fax or e-mail presentations should be made only when face-to-face presentations are not practical. Forty-seven states have adopted the Uniform Electronic Transactions Act, which gives legal recognition to electronic signatures.

When you take a listing from out-of-area owners, you should ascertain their fax number. If they don't have a fax, obtain the number that can be used at a local office service center such as Kinko's. Call or e-mail the owners to let them know the fax has been sent.

Purchase Offer Transmittal #2

UR
H O M E   R E A L T Y

FAX

Date: _____

To: _____

Attn: _____

From: _____

Pages w/cover: _____

Dear _____ :

I have enclosed an offer we have received on your property at [5874 Greenview Lane]. The offer is not what we had hoped it would be. You now have the following three options:

- Accept it. This would form a binding contract, and your home would be sold.

- Reject it outright. This would end the negotiation process.

- Make a counteroffer. You should realize that once a counteroffer is made, you can no longer accept the earlier offer because that offer is considered dead. The buyers then have the option of accepting or rejecting your counteroffer.

If you feel you can't risk losing this buyer, I would recommend accepting the offer rather than making a counteroffer. I have enclosed a seller's net proceeds estimate based on the offer. If you can take the risk, I would recommend a counteroffer of [$430,000], although the amount of the counteroffer is your decision.

Besides the acceptance, which can be enacted by your signature, I have also prepared a counteroffer reflecting my recommendations. Please sign and fax me the applicable forms as soon as possible. Keep in mind that a buyer can withdraw an offer without penalty anytime prior to being notified of its acceptance.

Call me at [800-555-1111] as soon as you receive this fax so I can go through the offer with you and answer any questions you may have.

Yours truly,

_____

Note: See notes on the previous fax transmittal letter.

Purchase Offer Transmittal/Full Price

UR
H O M E   R E A L T Y

FAX

Date:_____

To:_____ Attn:_____

From:_____ Pages w/cover:_____

I am proud to enclose a full-price purchase offer from [Janet Smith]. [The only deviation from your requirement is that (Ms. Smith) has requested a 60-day closing period.]

Before [1. he   2. she] is notified of your acceptance, [Ms. Smith] could conceivably revoke her offer; therefore, please sign and fax your acceptance, where indicated, immediately.

Please call me at [(800) 555-1111] when you receive this fax so that I can explain the offer and answer any questions you may have.

Yours truly,

_____

Note: An immediate notification that a fax is on its way should be made by phone or e-mail. See notes with previous fax messages.

Poor Offer Transmittal

UR
H O M E   R E A L T Y

FAX

To:_____

From:_____

Date:_____

Attn:_____

Pages w/cover:_____

Dear _____:

As your agent, I am required to submit every offer received. I am therefore transmitting the enclosed purchase offer.

I recommend that rather than an outright rejection of this offer, we counter [1. with a price of ($419,000) 2. excluding the furnishings from the sale].

Although you have the right to accept the offer and form a binding contract, I hope that you will follow my advice; I do not think an acceptance of the offer as presented would be in your best interest.

Please call me at [(800) 555-1111] as soon as you receive this fax.

Yours truly,

_____

Note: If the offer revealed specific problems, such as dangerous clauses like subordination agreements, or if the offer involved unsecured notes or trades of property having questionable value, you should specifically point out these problems. See notes with previous fax messages.

Seller Net Proceeds Estimate—After Offer

UR
H O M E   R E A L T Y

_____ ← Date and address

_____
_____
_____

Dear _____:

Enclosed is a seller net proceeds worksheet that I have prepared for your property, based on the purchase offer price of [**$419,000**].

I believe these figures are reliable but they are not guaranteed.

If you have any questions, please call me.

Yours truly,

_____

Enclosure: ← Card, seller net proceeds worksheet

Note: See page 150 for enclosure. Normally this would be covered when the offer was presented for acceptance.

Offer Rejected

UR
H O M E   R E A L T Y

_____ ← Date and address

_____
_____
_____

Dear _____:

I'm very sorry the offer we received on your [1. home 2. property 3. lot] failed to meet your expectations. As your agents, we have a duty to present every offer received.

I want you to know that we will continue with our best efforts to sell your [1. home 2. property 3. lot], and we remain hopeful of an early success.

Yours truly,

_____

Enclosure: ← Card

Status of Sale

To:

From: agent@urhome.com

Subject: Financing Approved!

Dear _____:

Congratulations! [The financing has been approved] for [1. Janet Jones   2. the Joneses   3. the purchaser(s) of your (home)].

I will be contacting you in a few days to give you closing information.

Yours truly,

_____

Note: E-mail messages would be preferable to letters as to status of sale. Owners are anxious to know what is happening about their financing.

Removal of Contingency

To:

From: agent@urhome.com

Subject: Contingency Removed

Attachment(s):   Contingency Release

Dear _____:

This is to inform you that [the Joneses] have signed the attached contingency release. Their purchase agreement now stands without the contingency [of obtaining a 6 percent loan for 80 percent of the purchase price].

[We should be able to close the sale by (November 1).]

Yours truly,

_____

Note: See note on prior letter.

Failure of Buyer Contingency

UR
HOME REALTY

_____ ← Date and address

_____
_____
_____

Dear _____:

As I explained [1. in our phone conversation 2. in my e-mail message], [Mr. and Mrs. Brown] have been unable to [1. obtain financing 2. qualify] according to the contingency set forth in their purchase offer.

Please sign and return the enclosed release forms so that I can return their deposit in accord with our agreement.

We have resumed our sales efforts and are confident of success in selling your home.

Yours truly,

_____

Enclosure: ← Card, release form, prepaid overnight delivery envelope

---

Note: When it appears a contingency will not be met, inform the owner immediately via phone or e-mail so that failure will not come as a shock. Be certain that the seller agrees to the return of the deposit before it is returned. Otherwise, a court could later decide that the failure to meet the contingency was the fault of the buyer. If this is the case, you could be held liable for the returned deposit. For a release, use either a standard form or have an attorney prepare one for you.

Closing Documents Transmittal—To Buyer or Seller

UR
H O M E   R E A L T Y

_____ ⟵ Date and address

_____
_____
_____

Dear _____:

Enclosed are the following documents for [1. your signature   2. both of your signatures]:

_____
_____
_____
_____

Please sign where indicated.

[Important: _____
_____

and _____
must be signed in the presence of a notary public.]

Please return the documents as indicated by [10 June].

Yours truly,

_____

Enclosure: ⟵ Card, [closing statement, deed, mortgage, disclosures] and prepaid
                    envelope

Note: Ordinarily you should have the buyer and the seller come to your office or escrow office to sign documents. A letter would likely be used only when a party is not in the area. If mailed, use an overnight service that emphasizes the importance of the material, and include a similar prepaid return envelope. You should phone or e-mail the party that the material is on its way.

Closing Status—To Buyer or Seller

UR
H O M E   R E A L T Y

_____ ← Date and address

_____
_____
_____

Dear _____:

The closing of your [1. home sale 2. home purchase] [1. should be on schedule
2. is earlier than expected 3. is delayed because (state reasons); I will inform you as
soon as this is resolved].

[1. We do not anticipate any problems with the closing. 2. If we encounter any
problems, we will notify you immediately.]

If you have any questions, please contact me.

Yours truly,

_____

Enclosure: ← Card

Note: If there is a problem or delay of any kind, the parties should preferably be
notified immediately by phone, e-mail, or fax.

Notice of Closing

UR
H O M E   R E A L T Y

_____ ← Date and address

_____

_____

_____

The closing for the sale of your home at [2713 Plymouth Street] will take place at [our Wells Street office at 9 AM] on [August 6]. [The seller must be present.] The following checklist may be helpful to you:

Seller's Checklist

☐ Notify the post office of your change of address.

☐ Notify magazines, credit card companies, banks, motor vehicle department, insurance companies, friends, and so on, of your address change.

☐ Notify homeowners' association of sale and new owner.

☐ Cancel subscriptions to newspapers, or let them know of your change of address.

☐ Cancel or arrange to transfer service contracts such as pest control, gardener, or water softener company.

☐ Cancel or transfer any homeowners' insurance coverage as of the closing date.

☐ Disconnect or transfer utilities on final reading.

  ☐ Water

  ☐ Gas

  ☐ Electricity

  ☐ Phone

  ☐ Internet

  ☐ Cable TV

  ☐ Trash

☐ Leave all warranties and manuals for appliances.

(1)

---

(1)

☐ Leave extra keys.

☐ Leave garage door openers, gate openers or cards, pool passes, as appropriate.

If you have any questions concerning the closing, please contact me.

Yours truly,

_____

Enclosure: ⟵ Card

Note: If the sellers must be present for closing, you should call them several days in advance to make certain they will be present.

Settlement Statement Transmittal

UR
HOME REALTY

_____ ← Date and address

_____
_____
_____

Dear _____:

Enclosed is your check for [$207,812.69], as well as your settlement statement for the sale of your property at [77 Lynn Court].

We hope to be able to serve you for any future real estate needs.

Yours truly,

_____

Enclosure: ← Card, check, settlement statement

Note: Normally, an independent escrow agent or an attorney would handle this. In some areas, brokers may act as escrow. Whenever possible, present checks in person. This gives you several opportunities: you can discuss an owner's future plans, ask for referrals, and request a testimonial letter. A letter like this should be sent by certified mail.

Closing Statement Question—Buyer or Seller

UR
HOME REALTY

_____ ← Date and address

_____
_____
_____

Dear _____:

In regard to your [1. letter of (June 8) 2. telephone call on (June 8)], I have reviewed your closing statement for [1531 Rockwell Street].

[You are absolutely correct that an error was made, and I apologize for not discovering it. (1. I have enclosed a corrected statement and a check for ($30.50). 2. The escrow office will be sending you a corrected closing statement and a check.)]

[The document preparation charge was for preparation of the warranty deed and the second mortgage and note. The charge of ($40) is a reasonable charge for this service.]

[The charge for title insurance is based on (paragraph 16) of the purchase contract whereby you agreed to provide this policy. It is also normal for the seller to pay for a standard policy of title insurance and the buyer to pay for any extended coverage desired.]

I will be calling you in the next few days to make certain that you fully understand the closing statement and to answer any other questions you might have.

If you have any further questions or if I can be of service to you in any way, please do not hesitate to contact me.

Sincerely,

_____

Enclosure: ← Card

Request for Return of Personal Property

UR
HOME REALTY

_____ ← Date and address

_____

_____

_____

Dear _____:

The [Smiths] are now in their new home and are delighted with it. [You certainly took excellent care of this fine home.]

We do have a minor problem: The [dining room ceiling fan] was not in the house when the [Smiths] took possession. Your movers might have inadvertently packed it. As you realize, [1. the purchase contract called for the ceiling fan to stay 2. the listing made a positive point of the ceiling fan remaining 3. the ceiling fan is regarded as a fixture, which must be left with the house unless agreed otherwise].

Please pack and return the [ceiling fan] to the [Smiths] as soon as practical. Thank you in advance for your prompt attention to this matter.

Yours truly,

_____

cc: [Smiths]

Note: This is a diplomatic letter asking for the return of an item. Ordinarily, a problem such as this occurs when the seller has not vacated at the time of closing, so the walk-through would not have revealed that the property was taken.

Thank You to Buyer or Seller #1

UR
H O M E   R E A L T Y

_____ ← Date and address

_____
_____
_____

Dear _____:

I would like to thank you for letting me serve you in the [1. sale 2. purchase] of your home. [1. I am certain your new home will bring your family much happiness. 2. Based on the current market, I believe that the (1. sale 2. purchase) was very advantageous to you.]

If I can be of any service to you in meeting your future real estate needs, do not hesitate to contact me. If you are happy with my services, I hope that you will recommend me to your friends.

Best wishes,

_____

Enclosure: ← Card

Thank You to Buyer or Seller #2

UR

H O M E   R E A L T Y

_____ ← Date and address

_____
_____
_____

Dear _____:

Just a note to say thank you [1. for entrusting the sale of your home to me   2. for allowing me to help you buy your new home].

All too often in today's rush of doing business, we forget to say thanks. But not this time. I have enjoyed fulfilling your needs. If I can ever do anything else for you, please let me know.

Best wishes,

_____

Enclosure: ← Card

Move-In Gift to Buyer

UR
H O M E   R E A L T Y

_____ ← Date and address

_____
_____
_____

Dear _____:

I know you will enjoy your new home. I have enclosed a little housewarming gift [an indoor/outdoor digital thermometer] as a small measure of my thanks for entrusting me to aid you in the purchase of your new home.

I wish you many years of happiness at [1122 Sunset Lane].

Yours truly,

_____

Note: A handwritten note would be more appropriate than a typed note.

Service Evaluation—To Seller After Sale

UR

H O M E   R E A L T Y

_____ ⟵ Date and address

_____
_____
_____

Dear _____:

To improve our service to sellers, we would appreciate very much if you would rate the services of [UR Home Realty] in the sale of your home.

Seller Evaluation of [UR Home Realty]

1. Do you feel that the listing agent understood your needs and concerns?
   ☐ Yes ☐ No

2. Do you feel that the listing agent accurately described the services we would provide?   ☐ Yes ☐ No

3. Do you feel that the listing agent was realistic in making recommendations for a listing price?   ☐ Yes ☐ No

4. Did the listing agent make recommendations to you about the property, showings, and open houses to increase the likelihood of a sale?   ☐ Yes ☐ No

5. Do you feel that you were kept adequately informed about our efforts on your behalf, as well as about what was happening in the market?   ☐ Yes ☐ No

6. Do you feel that the agent was fair and honest in presenting the offer and the recommendations made?   ☐ Yes ☐ No

7. During the period between acceptance of the purchase offer and the closing, do you feel that you were kept adequately informed as to what was happening?
   ☐ Yes ☐ No

8. Would you recommend our firm to friends who need to sell their home?
   ☐ Yes ☐ No

(1)

(2)

9. Can we use your name as a satisfied seller or allow other owners to see your evaluation of [UR Home Realty]?   ☐ Yes ☐ No

10. We would appreciate your suggestions on how we can improve our services.

_____

_____

_____

_____

Please return this evaluation in the enclosed stamped envelope. Thank you for your time and consideration.

Yours truly,

[John Jones]

[Broker, UR Home Realty]

Enclosure: ⟵ Card, self-addressed stamped envelope

Note: Negative responses identify weaknesses so that greater effort can be expended in the future. Positive responses provide you with an excellent listing tool.

Buyer or Seller Request for Testimonial Letter

UR
H O M E   R E A L T Y

_____ ← Date and address

_____
_____
_____

Dear _____:

I enjoyed working with you, and I am pleased that we were successful in [1. the sale of your home   2. finding the house that has become your new home].

Many [1. sellers   2. buyers] are influenced by the experiences of others in choosing a real estate agent to work with. If you could send me a letter describing how you view my services, it would be of great help to me.

I thank you for your confidence in working with me and hope you think of me should you have future real estate needs.

All the best,

_____

Enclosure: ← Card, self-addressed stamped envelope

Thank You for Testimonial Letter

UR
HOME REALTY

_____ ← Date and address

_____
_____
_____

Dear _____:

Thank you so much for your kind letter. I am so pleased that you were happy with my services.

I will do my best to live up to the image you have given me in meeting any future real estate needs you might have. I am honored to have helped you in [1. buying 2. selling] your home.

All the best,

_____

Enclosure: ← Card

Notification to Seller of Referral

UR
H O M E   R E A L T Y

_____ ← Date and address

_____
_____
_____

Dear _____:

I am delighted that we were able to find a buyer for your home, but I am sad you will be leaving our community. Unfortunately, sometimes in real estate sales, you form relationships with people who intend to move away. However, I wish you great happiness in [Richmond].

To help you meet your housing needs, I have contacted [Tom Smith] of [Smith Realty] in [Richmond]. [(Tom) is a buyer's agent who has a duty to meet and protect the interests of buyers.] [Because I think (Tom) can help you, I gave (Tom) your e-mail address. He will be contacting you to ascertain your specific housing needs.] [I suggest you call (Tom) at (800-760-2222) to go over your specific housing needs.] [(Tom) can send you information and photos of available homes, as well as provide Web site information so you can presearch for the perfect home.] [Both our offices and (Smith Realty) are members of (Worldwide Referrals). It is a cooperative organization of over (1,800) real estate professionals concerned with meeting the relocation needs of homeowners.] I have also contacted the [Richmond] Chamber of Commerce, and they will be sending you area information and maps.

If I can ever be of service to you again, please don't hesitate to contact me.

Your friend,

_____

Enclosure: ← Card

BUYER E-MAILS AND LETTERS

Unsolicited e-mail solicitations must include an opt-out mechanism, as well as the physical location of the sender.

New Listing [Brookside] Area

To:

From: agent@urhome.com

Subject: New listing—Meets your criteria

Dear _____:

New on the market [today] this [3-bedroom, 2½-bath, newer colonial] in [Brookside] is priced at [$239,000].

From your indicated preferences, it appears [we have found your new home]; [to be what you have been seeking in a new home]; [to be a home you would be interested in viewing].

Check attachments for photo(s) and property details.

Contact me by e-mail at *agent@urhome.com.*

UR Home Realty

2817 Main Street

Northland, IL 60620-2934

Cell phone: 602-555-8200

   Or: 800-555-1111

☐ I no longer wish to receive alerts about homes being placed on the market.

Property Inquiry E-mail #1

To:	
From:	agent@urhome.com
Subject:	Requested Property Information
Attachment(s):	Property Information Sheet

Dear _____ :

The [1 1 1 Midvale Lane] property that you have inquired about offers a very special opportunity. Although you really must see the property in person to fully appreciate it, I have attached a descriptive sheet for you. You can also [1. view the property 2. take a virtual tour of the property] by visiting our Web site at [www.urhome.com] and clicking on [Inventory #37A].

I will be calling you to answer any questions you may have and to tell you about several other properties that might be of interest to you.

Yours truly,

_____

Note: The purpose of the call would be to set up a definite time to show the property. A phone call to obtain e-mail address would be proper so that the party can receive information in a timely manner.

Property Inquiry E-mail #2

To:	
From:	agent@urhome.com
Subject:	Requested Property Information
Attachment(s):	Property Information Sheets

Dear _____:

I am very happy to send you the material that you requested on the [30 acres and 2 houses] advertised in the [Sunday Daily Ledger].

[I think you will get a better appreciation of this opportunity by viewing our Web site, (www.urhome.com). You can click on ("Inventory" and check "Homes with Acreage").]

[I have also included information on several similar properties that are available.] I will call you so we can arrange for you to view [1. this   2. these] rare opportunities.

Yours truly,

_____

Note: The purpose of the call would be to set up a definite time to show the property. See notes with previous e-mail.

Out-of-Area Housing Inquiry

To:	
From:	agent@urhome.com
Subject:	Requested Property Information
Attachment(s):	Property Information Sheets

Dear _____:

I will be happy to help you find a [3-bedroom, 2-bath home with at least one acre of land] in the [Brookfield area] within the [$300,000–$350,000] price range you have indicated.

I have included descriptive information about some properties that I think might interest you. Our Web site, [www.ur-home.net], will provide you with information, photos, and even virtual tours of these, as well as additional properties.

I will be calling you to answer any questions you may have and to discuss any features you consider desirable for your future home, as well as to arrange a convenient time to show you our community and, hopefully, your next home.

Yours truly,

_____

Note: A preferred approach would be a phone call to discuss housing needs.

Out-of-Area Buyer—Notice of Properties of Interest

To:

From: agent@urhome.com

Subject: [Two] Just Available Homes

Attachment(s):   Property Information

Dear _____:

I want to make you aware of [two] recently available properties that I feel will be of great interest to you.

[1823 West Winter Place is a 4-year-old Williamsburg Colonial with 4 bedrooms, a den, 3½ baths, and a 3-car garage on a well-landscaped one-half acre site in a prestigious location. List price is $750,000, although I think there is may be negotiation room.]

[17415 62nd Boulevard is an older Victorian of magnificent proportions that has been totally updated. There are 5 bedrooms, 4 full baths, and 2 half-baths, a separate 2-bedroom, 1-bath suite above the 4-car garage, and it's set on more than an acre. The property is in probate and is listed at $895,000 with any offer subject to court approval.]

I think it would be in your best interests to come to [Cleveland] at your earliest convenience to view these opportunities. [You can (1. view 2. tour) these properties on our Web site, (www.urhome.com), by clicking on Inventory #47 and Inventory #51.]

Yours truly,

Note: An e-mail also provides an opportunity to include a virtual tour. If none is available, you can create one yourself using a digital camera (check www.visualtour. com, one of several programs available). If you must use a letter, it should be sent via an overnight delivery service to express urgency. It is essential that when you ask an out-of-area buyer to come quickly to view a property, you are reasonably certain the property will be what the buyer wants based on conversations and/or prior property showings. If the prospective buyer is not interested in the property, your credibility will suffer and you could lose a valued prospective buyer.

Request for Buyer Information

To:	
From:	agent@urhome.com
Subject:	Requested Information – Homes In [Hortonville]
Attachment(s):	Prospective Buyer Confidential Information

Dear _____:

To best meet your housing needs, I would appreciate it if you could complete the attached Prospective Buyer Confidential Information Form.

Although some of the questions may seem personal, the information you provide will help us to understand your needs. This is really the first step toward locating a new home for you and your family.

To aid your home search and to allow you to negotiate from a position of strength, you will want to be preapproved for a home loan. You can complete the application for approval on our Web site, [www.URHomeRealty/FinancialQualifying].

Yours truly,

_____

Prospective Buyer Confidential Information Form

UR

HOME REALTY

Prospective Buyer Confidential Information

Name(s):_____   Home Phone:_____

E-mail:_____   Cell Phone:_____

Address:_____   Fax (if available):_____

Size of family: _____

Names and ages of children or other dependents living with you:

_____   _____

_____   _____

_____   _____

Initial contact with this firm was motivated by (advertisement, sign, referral, etc.):

_____

Present address: _____

How long at above address? _____

Do you presently own your own home?   ☐ Yes ☐ No

If yes, must you sell before you buy?   ☐ Yes ☐ No

If yes, is your present home currently listed for sale?   ☐ Yes ☐ No

With: _____

Your reason(s) for buying a new home: _____

_____

How long have you been looking for a new home? _____

Have you found any home that you like?   ☐ Yes ☐ No

If yes, why didn't you purchase? _____

_____

(1)

(2)

Areas or locations that are of special interest to you: _____

_____

_____

Why? _____

_____

_____

Do you currently own all your own appliances (stove, refrigerator, washer/dryer)?

_____

What features do you like about your present home? _____

_____

_____

Why? _____

_____

_____

Do you have a pet?   ☐ Yes ☐ No   What kind? _____

Do you have any special needs such as handicapped-accessible?   ☐ Yes ☐ No

Describe these requirements: _____

_____

List the special features you desire in a new home:	Must Have	Desired
_____	☐	☐
_____	☐	☐
_____	☐	☐
_____	☐	☐
_____	☐	☐
_____	☐	☐
_____	☐	☐
_____	☐	☐
_____	☐	☐

What are your hobbies or special interests? _____

_____

Have you qualified for or been turned down for a home loan within the past year?

_____

If you qualified for a loan, what was the name of the firm and loan amount?

_____

(3)

Approximate monthly gross income (before taxes and other deductions): $ _____
Total monthly payments on long-term debt (one year or more revolving credit accounts plus car, etc.): $ _____

What are you willing to invest toward a down payment on a home? $ _____

This form will be kept in a confidential prospective buyer file by

[UR Home Realty]

[602-555-8200]

[agent@urhome.com]

Note: This form could be used as a mailing or e-mail attachment or delivered in person to determine housing needs and financial qualification.

Buyer Monthly Costs Estimate Worksheet

UR
H O M E   R E A L T Y

_____ ← Date and address

_____
_____
_____

Dear _____:

I have prepared the following estimate of the true monthly costs of home ownership for [the home at 387 Elm Street] considering the tax benefits offered by home ownership.

The estimate is based on the following assumptions:

Purchase price	[$295,000]
Total closing costs	[$4,000]
Down payment	[$60,000]
Amount to be financed	[$239,000]

[30-year fixed-rate] loan at [6%] interest

Estimated Gross Monthly Costs

Principal and interest	[$1,432.92]
Property tax	[$375.00]
Homeowners' insurance	[$42.00]
Other [association dues]	[$60.00]
Total estimated monthly gross costs	[$1,909.92]

Tax Benefits (Monthly)

Estimated deductible interest	[$1,195.00]
Estimated deductible property tax	[$375.00]
Monthly total tax deductions	[$1,570.00]
Estimated tax bracket (federal + state)	[34%]
[$1,570] × [34%] = monthly tax benefit	[$533.80]

(1)

(2)

Estimated Net Monthly Costs

Estimated gross monthly cost   [$1,909.92]

Minus Estimated monthly tax benefits [−$533.80]

Monthly cost adjusted for tax benefits [$1,375.12]

Although these costs are estimates only, I have tried to be as realistic as possible, and I believe that actual costs will not vary significantly from this estimate.

I will be calling you to discuss the estimate [and to arrange showings of homes that I believe will interest you].

Yours truly,

_____

Enclosure: ⟵ Card

Note: You should prepare the buyer's monthly costs estimate worksheet as a form to use during a buyer qualifying session. This letter could be an e-mail or used as an attachment to an e-mail.

Prospective Buyer—New Listing

To:	
From:	agent@urhome.com
Subject:	Fantastic New Listing
Attachment(s):	New Listing

Dear _____:

[I was unable to reach you by phone, but I wanted to let you know that] we have just accepted a new listing that I believe is exactly what you have been looking for. I want you to see this very special home before it is advertised to the general public.

Please call me at once. I wouldn't want you to miss this opportunity!

Yours truly,

_____

Note: This is preferable as an e-mail. If you need to send a letter, use overnight delivery. This message creates a sense of urgency and sets a buying, rather than looking, mood. No information is given because if it included anything buyers considered negative, they would not be eager to see the property. You can continue the tone of urgency by asking prospective buyers whether they can take time off from work to see it. If they like the house, they will be happy they did. Warning: Be reasonably certain that this is the house for your clients, or your credibility could be damaged.

E-mail Alert

To:	
From:	agent@urhome.com
Subject:	E-mail Alert—New Property on Market
Attachment(s):	Photo

Dear _____:

The [4-year-old, 3-bedroom, 2½-bath, center hall colonial] at [6722 Edgemont] in [Orchard Ridge] has come on the market today. It is listed at [$347,900].

[Photo and Details]

Please reply to this message if you would like to be the first to see this fine property.

If any of your friends would like to receive these e-mail alerts, have them e-mail or call me.

[UR Home Realty]

[602-555-8200]

[John Davis]

Note: Whenever you receive an inquiry about property, you should ask the prospective buyers whether they would like to receive e-mail alerts of new listings that meet their criteria as soon as they are received and before the property is advertised to the public. Most callers will like to have this advantage and will readily provide their e-mail addresses. By including a photo in the e-mail as well as some basic details, you do not have to wait until a descriptive property sheet is prepared to alert prospective buyers.

Prospective Buyer—Price Reduction

To:

From: agent@urhome.com

Subject: Home You Liked—Price Reduction

Dear _____:

The house you liked so much in [Elmside], the one with [the huge fireplace and the fruit trees in the backyard], has just been reduced in price. The original price set by the owners was [$269,500], but they have reduced this to [$237,000], a net reduction of [$32,500].

This reduction should result in a very quick sale. Because I would hate to see anyone else get this exceptional buy, I think you should take another look at this property. I will call you to arrange a showing of this home and another new listing that I think will interest you.

Yours truly,

_____

Note: While an initial phone call would be preferable, this e-mail would be appropriate for a prospective buyer who has been unreachable by phone. Send this e-mail if the prospects indicated any interest. The mention of the other home is a final hook to set up the showings.

Cover Letter, Offer to Purchase (Out-of-Area Buyer)

UR
H O M E   R E A L T Y

_____ ⟵ Date and address

_____
_____
_____

Dear _____:

As we discussed on the phone on [Wednesday, October 8], I have prepared a purchase offer for the property at [1 1 1 Midvale Lane] as you directed. The purchase offer reflects your offering price of [$265,000], and it includes [1. terms 2. items that vary from the listing, and any special conditions].

Please sign and return [three] copies of the purchase agreement to me as soon as possible, along with [your deposit check for $10,000], [which will be held uncashed until the offer is accepted]. If the offer is not accepted, your deposit will be returned to you in full.

If the owners accept your offer, I believe that you will have made an exceptionally fine purchase. [Even at the list price, I think this home is an excellent buy.]

Call me at [800-555-1 1 1 1] as soon as you receive this package so I can go over the purchase offer with you and answer any questions you may have.

Yours truly,

_____

Enclosures: ⟵ Card, offer to purchase, return envelope

Note: While a fax is preferable, if a letter is used, the letter should be sent by an overnight delivery service such as FedEx, and a paid envelope should be included for similar return service. If you wish to have the signed offer returned by fax, instruct the buyer to send the earnest money deposit by wire transfer. Notify the listing agent that an offer is coming. You do not want the owner to accept another offer while your offer is in transit.

Offer to Purchase (Out-of-Area Buyer)

UR

H O M E   R E A L T Y

FAX

To: _____

From: _____

Date: _____

Attn: _____

Pages w/cover: _____

RE: Offer to Purchase

Dear _____:

Attached is the purchase offer for the property at [I I I Midvale Lane] that I have prepared as you directed in our telephone conversation on [Wednesday, October 8].

Please call me at [800-555-I I I I] as soon as you have read the offer so I can answer any questions you may have.

Please fax the signed offer to me. I will explain how you should wire transfer your earnest money deposit to our trust account.

Awaiting your call,

Agent@urhome.com

UR Home Realty

2817 Main Street

Northland, IL 60620-2934

Cell phone: 602-555-8200

   Or: 800-555-1111

Fax: 615-820-7737

Notification of Offer Acceptance

To:

From: agent@urhome.com

Subject: Offer Accepted! You Have a New Home!

Dear _____:

I am pleased to inform you that your offer for the purchase of the property at [55 Chestnut Street] has been accepted without qualification. [1. Attached is the signed acceptance. 2. I have (mailed) (faxed) the signed acceptance.]

[As your agent], I will work with you throughout the closing process.

I congratulate you on your wonderful purchase.

Sincerely,

_____

Note: The preferred method of notification is in person. If this is not possible, make the notification by phone or e-mail, indicating that the acceptance has been mailed via an overnight delivery service or faxed. The copy of the acceptance can be an attachment to the e-mail.

Rejection of Offer—No Counteroffer (Recommend New Full-Price Offer)

To:	
From:	agent@urhome.com
Subject:	New Offer
Attachment(s):	Offer to Purchase

Dear _____:

[As we discussed on the phone], [Mr. and Mrs. Jones] have indicated that they are unable to accept your offer to purchase their [home]. Although they would very much like to sell to you, they feel that the price they had set is more than reasonable based on the current real estate marketplace.

Because I feel very strongly that this [home] meets your needs better than any other [home] available and that the price asked is favorable, I have enclosed a new offer form reflecting that price.

If you wish to be the owner of this wonderful [home], please sign and return [three] copies of the offer in the envelope provided. [It would be unfortunate to lose this fine opportunity for a difference of only about 5 percent.]

I will call you to answer any questions that you might have.

Yours truly,

_____

P.S. Keep in mind that long after the price has been forgotten, you will be enjoying the [1. amenities 2. advantages] of this fine [home].

Note: If at all possible, prospective buyers should be immediately notified by phone, e-mail, or in person of a rejection of their offer. A personal notification would be preferable.

Notice to Buyer of Seller Counteroffer (Recommend Acceptance)

UR
H O M E   R E A L T Y

_____ ← Date and address

_____
_____
_____

Dear _____:

[Mr. and Mrs. Smith], the owners of the property at [8712 Mayville Lane], have presented a counter to your offer to purchase their home. The changes they have made are as follows:

1. [Price to be $529,000 rather than the $499,000 price that you offered.]

2. [Closing to be in 60 days rather than the 30 days that you indicated.]

[At the time of your offer, I indicated that a price of ($499,000) was probably a little low based on comparables.] [The list price of ($559,000) was not unreasonable, but your offer has resulted in a counteroffer giving you a ($30,000) reduction from the list price.]

I believe that the counteroffer of [$529,000] is still an excellent purchase opportunity and recommend your acceptance of the counteroffer.

Please sign and fax a copy of your acceptance of the counteroffer to me at [760-200-8888] and mail [three] copies of the signed acceptance to me.

Until this counteroffer is accepted, the owners have the right to revoke this counteroffer.

Sincerely,

_____

Enclosures: ← Card, three copies of counteroffer, self-addressed stamped envelope

---

Note: If presentation in person is not possible, the buyers should be notified by phone or e-mail of the counteroffer. They can then fax acceptance of the stated changes. As an alternative approach, you could send this letter by fax, overnight service, or e-mail with a counteroffer attached. By showing the buyers that their negotiations gave them a discount from the list price, you increase the likelihood of acceptance. Never recommend a counteroffer acceptance that you do not believe to be in the best interests of the buyers.

Buyer Purchase Cost Estimate

To:	
From:	agent@urhome.com
Subject:	Buyer Cost Estimate
Attachment(s):	Worksheet

Dear _____:

Attached is our Buyer Cost Estimate Worksheet. While we believe that the estimates are reasonably reliable, they are not guaranteed.

If you have any questions, please call me.

Yours truly,

_____

Note: The Buyer Cost Estimate Worksheet is on page 217.

Buyer Cost Estimate Worksheet

UR
H O M E   R E A L T Y

Buyer Cost Estimate Prepared for [John and Sara Smith]

Property: _____

Costs		Credits	
Purchase price	$ _____	Down payment	$ _____
Loan costs		Loans being assumed	($ _____)
Appraisal fee	$ _____	Seller financing	($ _____)
Origination costs	$ _____	Taxes (prorated)	($ _____)
Miscellaneous fees	$ _____	Other	$ _____
Impound account	$ _____	**Total credits**	$ _____
Buyer broker fee	$ _____		
Inspection costs	$ _____		
Insurance	$ _____		
Taxes (prorated)	$ _____		
Title insurance/abstracts	$ _____		
Attorney fees/escrow	$ _____		
Miscellaneous costs	$ _____		
Total costs	$ _____		
Total credits	($ _____)		
	$ _____	To be financed or paid at closing	

Waiver of Contingency Request

To:	
CC:	[Owner]
From:	agent@urhome.com
Subject:	Contingency in Offer
Attachment(s):	Waiver of Contingency Form

Dear _____:

Your offer-to-purchase agreement dated [August 11, 2012,] was contingent on [the sale of your home on Doyle Street].

The purchase contract provides that if a subsequent written offer is accepted that is contingent on your rights, you shall have [seven days] to waive the contingencies set forth in your offer. You are hereby notified that a subsequent offer has been received and accepted. Unless the seller receives notice by [September 14] that you have waived your contingencies, your offer shall terminate and become void, and your earnest money deposit will be returned to you. You are also advised that such notification must be prompt.

A contingency release form is attached for your signature. If you wish to waive the contingencies in your purchase offer, please sign where indicated and fax the release to me.

If you have any questions, please contact me immediately.

Yours truly,

_____

Note: A buyer who cannot be personally contacted should be notified immediately by phone and the contingency release form should be sent by e-mail or fax. The form should then be returned by fax. If mailed as a letter, it should be sent by express carrier.

Problem with a Contract Condition—Buyer or Seller

To:

CC: [1. Buyer 2. Seller]

From: agent@urhome.com

Subject: Condition of offer to be met

Attachment(s): Card

Dear _____:

As we agreed in our telephone discussion on [July 25], your purchase contract for the [1. purchase 2. sale] of [11475 Wedgewood Way] requires that [1. an 80 percent loan commitment 2. roof replacement] be [1. obtained 2. completed] by [August 1].

[1. You indicated 2. It is my understanding] that the above condition has not yet been fulfilled. You therefore are at risk of the [1. buyer 2. seller] declaring you in default of your agreement, [which might result in damages].

If there is any problem fulfilling the required condition, [or if I can be of any help to you], please contact me immediately so I can work with you toward a satisfactory solution.

Yours truly,

_____

Note: After a phone call, an e-mail, fax, or a letter should be used to document the problem. If there appears to be a problem, the other party should, of course, be notified.

Buyer Failed Contingency

UR

H O M E   R E A L T Y

_____ ← Date and address

_____
_____
_____

Dear _____:

Your offer dated [June 1, 2012,] to purchase the property at [2736 Wright Road in Newton Heights] was contingent on [your obtaining a $300,000 loan with $30,000 down by July 15]. You were unable to [obtain the required financing and have indicated that you are unable to waive the contingency]. Therefore, in accord with your purchase offer, your offer has become null and void.

With the concurrence of the owners, I am enclosing [UR Home Realty] trust account check no. [2933] in the amount of [$5,000], representing the full return of your earnest money deposit made with your offer to purchase.

If you have any questions or if I can serve you in any way, please contact me.

Yours truly,

_____

cc: [Owner's name]

Enclosures: ← Card, check

Note: This letter provides a written record of what should have been discussed by phone. Obtain the owner's concurrence in writing before earnest money is returned because of a failed contingency.

Information to New Owner

```
                        UR
            H O M E    R E A L T Y

_____  ← Date and address


_____
_____
_____

Dear _____:

To aid you in getting established in your new home, we have included a list of phone
numbers for utility hookups, [cable TV], [trash pickup], and [newspapers], as well as
some general area information that we believe will be useful to you. If [UR Home
Realty] can be of any further assistance to you, or if you know anyone with real estate
needs, please contact me.

Wishing you a great life in your new home,


_____


Enclosures: ← Card, lists, general information
```

Note: In addition to phone numbers, consider area maps, school information, information about houses of worship in the area, bus information, and so on. Your local chamber of commerce office probably can supply you with a large packet of information for the new resident.

Information on Utilities and Services

UR

H O M E   R E A L T Y

_____ ← Date and address

_____
_____
_____

Dear _____:

For your information, here are a few numbers that will help when you move into your new home:

- Telephone service _____
- Internet service providers _____
- Gas connection _____
- Electrical service _____
- Water _____
- Cable TV _____
- Newspaper _____
- Trash service _____
- School registration _____
- Emergency Numbers
    - Fire _____
    - Police _____
    - Ambulance _____
    - [Other] _____

If you like, I would be happy to give you my recommendations for everything from an auto mechanic to a [hairstylist].

Sincerely,

_____

Enclosure: ← Card [map, chamber of commerce information]

School Registration Information

To:	
From:	agent@urhome.com
Subject:	School Registration for [Madison and Ethan]

Dear _____:

I just wanted to remind you that you can register [Madison and Ethan] for [Midvale School starting July 10].

By registering early, you will avoid having to rush after you move into your new home. I am certain that you will have plenty of other things to keep you busy.

Best regards,

_____

Insurance Solicitation

UR

H O M E   R E A L T Y

_____ ← Date and address

_____
_____
_____

Dear _____:

The lender, [Midvale Savings and Loan], will require you to carry a fire policy on your new home in the amount of at least [$400,000]. We recommend that you consider a homeowners' policy in the amount of [$400,000], which would provide [$1,000,000] in liability coverage as well as insure your possessions up to [$100,000].

We also recommend replacement coverage that pays the full value of personal property, not just a depreciated value. Such coverage is available through your full-service insurance agent [or, if you like, we can write the policy through our office and supply a copy to the lender. A policy providing the coverage we have recommended would cost ($480 for one year) if written through our office, with (United Casualty). I have enclosed a brochure describing the policy].

I will be contacting you [1. to find out whether you want our office to handle the insurance for you 2. to check whether I can be of any help in obtaining insurance coverage].

Yours truly,

_____

Enclosures: ← Card, insurance brochure

Note: This letter applies if your office is also licensed as an insurance broker.

Inspection Recommendation

To:

From: agent@urhome.com

Subject: Home Inspection

Dear _____:

According to the purchase contract, you are allowed to have a professional inspection of your new home before closing.

I strongly recommend that you have such an inspection. If you would like, I can recommend several inspectors that previous buyers have been satisfied with.

Let me know when you would like to have the inspection so I can coordinate the time with [the owner's agent] [the owners].

Yours truly,

_____

Buyer—Final Inspection

To:

From: agent@urhome.com

Subject: Final Walk-Through Inspection

Dear _____:

In accord with your purchase agreement, I have arranged for you to conduct a final [walk-through inspection] of the property on [Tuesday, September 23, at 10 AM] to make certain that it has been maintained properly [and repairs have been completed as agreed].

[I will meet you at the property.] [You can, of course, bring a professional inspector with you.] If for any reason you are not going to be available at this time, please contact me as soon as possible.

Yours truly,

_____

Note: Purchase contracts customarily provide for the purchaser to have a professional inspection and to have a final walk-through inspection.

Buyer/Seller Notice of Settlement Conference

To:

From: agent@urhome.com

Subject: Settlement Conference

Attachment(s):   Settlement Statement

Dear _____:

The settlement conference for your [1. sale   2. purchase] of [1 1 1 Midvale Lane] has been scheduled for [June 1, 20XX,] at [55 Sycamore Place, Suite 3301].

[All (1. buyers   2. sellers) must attend so they can sign the (1. mortgage   2. deed).]

[Please bring a cashier's check in the amount of ($39,528). See the enclosed statement.]

I am glad that we have been able to fulfill your needs [and I look forward to seeing you at the closing].

Best regards,

_____

Note: The trend is for settlements to be handled by an independent escrow without buyers or sellers being present. Call the parties several days prior to closing to make certain they are aware of the settlement date and time.

Closing Statement Transmittal

UR
H O M E   R E A L T Y

_____ ← Date and address

_____
_____
_____

Dear _____:

Enclosed is a copy of the closing statement for your [1. sale of 2. purchase of] [6160 Jupiter Lane].

[I am certain that you will enjoy many happy years in your new home.] If you or your friends have any future real estate needs, I hope that you will think of me.

Sincerely,

_____

Enclosures: ← Card, closing statement

Note: If an escrow is used, the escrow company would send out the closing statement.

Service Evaluation—Buyer After Sale

UR
H O M E   R E A L T Y

_____ ← Date and address

_____
_____
_____

Dear _____:

To help us improve our service to buyers, we would appreciate it if you would rate our services in the purchase of your home at [54769 Wilbur Avenue].

Buyer Evaluation of [UR Home Realty]

1. Do you feel that the real estate agent listened to you and really understood your needs?   ☐ Yes ☐ No

2. Do you feel that the agent was realistic in explaining the financial qualifications and down payment requirements for the home you purchased?
    ☐ Yes ☐ No

3. Do you feel that the agent made efforts to find a home for you that best meets your needs?   ☐ Yes ☐ No

4. Was the agent knowledgeable about homes shown, neighborhoods, market conditions, and financing?   ☐ Yes ☐ No

5. Were calls to the agent or questions you raised promptly returned or answered to your satisfaction?   ☐ Yes ☐ No

6. Do you feel that the agent was honest in all dealings with you and helpful in preparing your purchase offer?   ☐ Yes ☐ No

7. After the acceptance of the offer, was the agent helpful in suggesting a lender or financing alternatives?   ☐ Yes ☐ No

8. Do you feel that the agent kept you adequately informed during the period from your offer until closing?   ☐ Yes ☐ No

9. Would you recommend the services of the agent to a friend who wanted to buy a home?   ☐ Yes ☐ No

(1)

(2)

10. Can we show this evaluation to other prospective buyers?   ☐ Yes ☐ No

11. If requested, would you be willing to write a short testimonial letter as to your relationship with [UR Home Realty]? (This letter would be shown to prospective buyers.)   ☐ Yes ☐ No

12. May we phone you in the future for information about your neighborhood and referrals?   ☐ Yes ☐ No

13. Any additional comments: _____

_____

_____

Signature _____

Please return this evaluation in the enclosed stamped envelope. Thank you very much for your assistance.

Note: Buyers usually develop a rapport with the selling agent. Because this is an evaluation of that agent, you will receive many "Yes" responses. With the buyers' approvals, an agent can show these evaluations to prospective buyers during the qualification process. Positive evaluations help sell the agent as someone who is very helpful to buyers. If buyers indicate they are willing to provide a testimonial letter, a letter should be requested. A folder of such letters can be very persuasive in obtaining buyer agency. Permission to phone may provide an exception to the do-not-call registry rules beyond 18 months.

Notice to Apply for Homeowner Tax Exemption

UR
H O M E   R E A L T Y

_____ ← Date and address

_____
_____
_____

Dear _____:

[California] offers a special property tax exemption for owner-occupied homes. You must, however, apply for this exemption by [April 15] for the [2013] tax year. I have enclosed [1. information on applying for the exemption   2. an exemption application] for your convenience. I would feel terrible if you did not receive the benefits to which you are entitled. If you have any questions, please contact me.

Sincerely,

_____

Enclosure: ← Card, (tax exemption application)

Note: In many states, a resident homeowner is entitled to special tax treatment, but the homeowner must apply for it. In many areas, the escrow process will include the homeowner tax exemption applications.

Insurance Solicitation—Mortgage Insurance

UR

H O M E   R E A L T Y

_____ ← Date and address

_____
_____
_____

Dear _____ :

I hope that you are enjoying your lovely new home. You might be interested in the enclosed brochure. It concerns a mortgage insurance policy that will pay off your mortgage if you die or will make the payments for you if you become disabled. Because of your concern for your family, please consider this plan.

The premiums based on your mortgage at your age of [39] come to only [$24] a [month, and the payments are guaranteed to remain the same for the life of the loan.]

I will be calling you in a few days to answer any questions you might have concerning this low-cost family protection.

Sincerely,

_____

Enclosure: ← Card, insurance brochure

Note: If you sell mortgage insurance, a good time to sell is after the home sale has been closed. Before the sale, buyers are concerned about all the expenses of closing, and they are more reluctant to take on new debt. Mortgage insurance is actually decreasing term life insurance.

Buyer Who Purchased Through Another Broker

UR

H O M E   R E A L T Y

_____ ← Date and address

_____
_____
_____

Dear _____:

Congratulations! I was very happy to learn that you had found the [home] that fulfills your needs. Although I am sorry I was unable to locate that [special home] for you, I do wish you happiness in your new [home]. From what I know of the area, I am certain that you made a wise choice.

If you need real estate assistance in the future, I hope you will think of me. I am ready to give my best efforts on your behalf.

Sincerely,

_____

Enclosure: ← Card

Note: This letter reestablishes the relationship for future referrals or dealings. Otherwise, the buyers might avoid the agent because they believe the agent is angry with them for going elsewhere. The buyer might have developed a better rapport with the agent who failed to make the sale than with the successful agent.

Anniversary of Purchase

UR
H O M E   R E A L T Y

_____ ← Date and address

_____
_____
_____

Dear _____:

Although it is hard to realize, we are celebrating your anniversary this week! On [June 1], it will be exactly [one] year since [1. I sold you your home 2. you purchased your home through our office]. I hope that your home has been good to you this past year.

I will call you in a few days to ask for your help in identifying any of your friends who might need real estate services.

Happy anniversary!

_____

Enclosure: ← Card

Note: A call after 18 months would require that the party not be listed on the do-not-call registry or that you have written permission to call for referrals.

BREACH OF CONTRACT AND OTHER CONFLICT COMMUNICATIONS

In most cases, the broker's first action when a conflict arises should be a phone call or a face-to-face meeting. A phone call or a meeting might immediately resolve the conflict.

Release of Listing

UR
H O M E   R E A L T Y

_____ ← Date and address

_____
_____
_____

Dear _____:

You have indicated [by your letter of April 3] that you no longer wish to have [UR Home Realty] represent you in the sale of [your home] at [2137 Northbridge Road].

Therefore, I have enclosed a release form that releases you and [UR Home Realty] from any and all obligations under [the exclusive-right-to-sell listing agreement dated (March 1, 2012),] and cancels said agreement.

Please endorse two copies of the enclosed release [where indicated] and return them to me in the enclosed stamped envelope. I will then sign them and return a copy to you.

Please note that paragraph [6J] of the listing still applies, and if you sell to any buyer whose name we provided to you in writing within [60 days] of cancellation of our agency agreement, then [UR Home Realty] is entitled to the full commission as set forth in our agreement.

I regret that we were unable to get your property under contract. Please call us if you have any questions or if we can be of service in any way in the future.

Yours truly,

_____

Enclosures: ← Card, release

Note: Use a listing release form either prepared by your attorney or one prepared by one of the real estate forms providers. Do not attempt to draft your own legal document. Many brokers prefer a release to a lawsuit for damages. You should notify other offices that have shown the property so you can list their prospects with the owners.

Response to Owner or Attorney—Cancellation of Listing

UR
H O M E   R E A L T Y

_____ ← Date and address

_____
_____
_____

Dear _____:

I received your [letter] dated [December 1, 2012], in which you unilaterally canceled the listing agreement of [October 12, 2012], on the property located at [78153 Towne Avenue].

[1. We have worked diligently toward the sale of said property and have been meeting our contractual obligations. Therefore, under paragraph (16A) of the listing, demand is hereby made for the agreed cancellation fee of ($15,000).]

[2. Although we have worked diligently toward the sale of the property, we do understand the unique circumstances involved and are willing to meet with you in the hope we can reach a mutually satisfactory settlement.]

[I will be contacting you so we can resolve this matter.]

Yours truly,

_____

Enclosure: ← Card

Note: Because of the time and cost involved in legal action, as well as the hard feelings it generates, it is often preferable to mutually agree to a settlement.

Demand for Commission—Owner's Action Prevents Sale

UR
H O M E   R E A L T Y

_____ ← Date and address

_____
_____
_____

Dear _____:

Pursuant to our [exclusive-agency-listing agreement] on your property at [18 West-wood Court], our office was successful in obtaining an offer on said property. You accepted this offer to purchase on [January 14, 2012].

A sale was not concluded because you [1. were unable to clear title   2. failed to comply with the condition that the roof be replaced   3. refused to complete the transaction].

Our office has fully complied with the terms of said listing agreement in obtaining a buyer who was ready, willing, and able to buy under the price and terms you agreed to.

I will be calling you [to arrange a meeting] to clarify why the sale failed and to settle any obligations.

Yours truly,

_____

Enclosure: ← Card

Note: This letter states the facts as you know them. You are seeking to meet with the owner and reach a settlement. If another office procured the buyer, the broker for that office should be involved. If an agreement cannot be worked out, then you should consider arbitration. (Many listing forms provide for binding arbitration.) Otherwise, you should consider turning the matter over to an attorney.

Demand for Commission—Owner Refuses Full-Price Offer

UR
H O M E   R E A L T Y

_____ ← Date and address

_____
_____
_____

Dear _____:

Under the terms of our [exclusive-listing agreement] dated [April 12, 2012], [UR Home Realty] worked diligently to obtain a buyer for your property at [6714 Freeport Avenue].

On [August 1, 2012] we presented you with a full-price offer of [$529,000] in full accord with the terms specified in the listing agreement. The buyer, [Jane Jones], was ready, willing, and able to complete the purchase.

You responded to said offer by [1. refusing to sell 2. countering the offer with a price greater than the listing price].

Under [paragraph 6] of our agreement, [UR Home Realty] is entitled to the commission of [$31,740] based on your refusal to sell under the terms of our agreement.

I will be calling you in the next few days [to arrange to meet with you] in order to discuss our future relationship and obligations.

Yours truly,

_____

Enclosure: ← Card

Note: A settlement might involve a payment of money and/or a new listing at a different price, terms, and/or commission. If another broker procured the full-price offer, then that broker should be involved in any settlement agreement. If the matter cannot be resolved to your satisfaction, legal services should be considered.

Owner Removes Property from Market—Listing Is Not Cancelled

UR
H O M E   R E A L T Y

_____ ← Date and address

_____
_____
_____

Dear _____:

By your request, we will no longer advertise or show your [home] at [38217 Lilac Avenue] for sale. We will also take down our sign and remove the property from our multiple listing service and all Internet sites.

However, the listing agreement, as agreed, will remain in full force and effect until the termination date of [January 15, 2013]. If you or anyone else sells the [house] while our agreement is in effect, we will be entitled to our full compensation under the terms of our [exclusive-right-to-sell listing].

If you later decide to sell your home, we hope that you will consider the services and courtesy we have shown you.

Yours truly,

_____

Enclosure: ← Card

Note: This is not a release. A release from the listing would allow the owner to sell without paying any commission. This letter offers you protection if the owners ask to be released with the intention of avoiding commission payment because they have secretly located a buyer. This letter should be sent registered mail, return receipt requested.

Commission Due—Owner Removes Property from Market

UR
HOME REALTY

_____ ← Date and address

_____
_____
_____

Dear _____:

In accord with an exclusive-agency agreement dated [May 14, 2012], [UR Home Realty] has been diligent in searching for a buyer for your property at [197641 141st Street].

On [September 12, 2012], before the expiration of the agency contract, you [informed this office that the property was no longer available for sale]. Under [paragraph 6B] of the contract, you agreed to pay [UR Home Realty] [1. 6 percent of the list price 2. the sum of $30,000] if you removed the property from the market [or otherwise made it unmarketable] before the expiration of our agreement.

I will be calling you [to arrange a meeting] so we can discuss the reason for withdrawing your property from the market and to settle any obligations that exist.

Yours truly,

_____

Enclosure: ← Card

Note: This letter establishes the owner's contractual obligation but indicates your desire for an amiable settlement. No threat is being made.

Buyer Breach of Purchase Agreement

UR
H O M E   R E A L T Y

_____ ← Date and address

_____
_____
_____

Dear _____:

According to your purchase agreement with [Julie Smith] dated [June 1, 2012], for the purchase of [555 Midvale Court], you were required to [increase your deposit by $10,000] no later than [August 3, 2012].

You have failed to meet your contractual obligation. Therefore, I have been authorized as the agent for [Julie Smith] to inform you that your failure is a material breach of your agreement. The seller hereby declares the above contract null and void based on said breach.

[1. Under said agreement, your deposit is to be forfeited as liquidated damages; please sign and return the enclosed forms authorizing the release of your deposit to the seller as liquidated damages. 2. Your breach has voided the contract.]

Yours truly,

_____

Enclosure: ← Card, release of deposit

cc: [Julie Smith]

Note: Do not send this letter without specific written authorization from the owners. Always check with your legal representative. Rights vary among states.

Purchase After Buyer Agency Expires

UR
_____
H O M E   R E A L T Y

_____ ← Date and address

_____
_____
_____

Dear _____:

On [September 14, 2012], you entered into an [exclusive-authorization-to-acquire property] agreement with [UR Home Realty]. In accordance with [paragraph 7B] of this agreement, we provided you with a list of properties to which we introduced you. This list, which was given to you on [December 10, 2012], included the [home] owned by [Morris Black] located at [7314 Elm Ridge Road] in [Middlebury].

On [December 20, 2012], you entered into a contract directly with [Mr. Black] to purchase his [home] for [$600,000]. The sale was completed on [January 15, 2012].

Paragraph [7B.3] of our agreement provides that [UR Home Realty] shall be entitled to our fee if you purchase a property that [we introduced] you to within [90 days] of the expiration of our [exclusive-right-to-acquire-property] agreement and we included the property on a list we provided to you [within three days of the expiration of our agreement]. Therefore, in accordance with our agreement, demand is made for the sum of [$18,000].

If you have any questions or desire a meeting, please contact me.

Yours truly,

_____

Enclosure: ← Card

Note: A more aggressive approach is called for when a buyer and a seller get together to cut the agent out of an earned fee. You should consider having your attorney send this letter. Consider sending this as a registered letter.

Demand for Commission—Sale After Listing Expires

UR

H O M E   R E A L T Y

_____ ← Date and address

_____
_____
_____

Dear _____:

On [September 14, 2012], which was [ten] days after the expiration of our [exclusive-right-to-sell] listing agreement for your property at [2211 Main Street], you sold said property to [Jason and Christie Lloyd] for the sum of [$740,000]. [No agent was involved in this transaction.]

In accordance with [paragraph 6A] of the listing agreement, our office provided you the names of [Jason and Christie Lloyd] in writing on [September 4, 2012]. [Our office showed the Main Street property to (Jason and Christie Lloyd) on (August 6, 2012, as well as on August 18, 2012) and they physically entered the property on both occasions.]

[Paragraph 6A of the listing] agreement provides that our office is entitled to [full commission] if a sale is made within [90] days of the expiration of the listing agreement to anyone we showed the property to and whose name we provided to you in writing [within three days of the expiration of the listing agreement].

A sale was made within the designated protection period after the expiration of the listing agreement to a buyer procured by our firm of which you were properly notified in writing. In accordance with [paragraph 6A.3 of our listing agreement], our office is entitled to the sum of [$44,400]. Demand is hereby made for the remittance of this amount.

Please call me if you have any questions [or would like to arrange a meeting].

Yours truly,

_____

Enclosure: ← Card

Note: This is also a case of the buyer and the seller getting together to attempt to cut the broker out of a fee. No threat is made, but the supported facts are laid out. If you have any doubt as to the fact that you were the procuring cause of the subsequent sale, you should check with your attorney. You might want to have this letter sent by your attorney. Consider sending this as a registered letter.

Notice to Builder of Defect

UR

H O M E   R E A L T Y

_____ ← Date and address

_____
_____
_____

Dear _____:

[Mr. and Mrs. Riley], who purchased your [Glenway] home at [8741 Royal Court] through our office, have informed us that [the roof leaks in five places]. They are very concerned about this matter. It would be greatly appreciated if this deficiency were promptly corrected. Small matters often become major problems if not taken care of quickly. More important, an unhappy buyer can detract from both our reputations.

I look forward to continued beneficial cooperation between our firms and continued success in selling your homes.

Yours truly,

_____

Enclosure: ← Card

cc: [Mr. and Mrs. Riley]

Note: This letter sells the benefits of solving the problem and is not threatening. The purpose is to help avoid legal action. It is assumed that the new owner has already made the builder aware of the problem. While this is a courtesy letter, should there be legal action, you could be drawn into a lawsuit. Attorneys often will spread a broad net, seeking deep pockets when claiming negligence. Therefore, you want to use any clout you have with the builder to resolve the problem. Dissatisfied buyers also have a negative effect on your firm's reputation, even if it is not your problem.

Official Inquiry—Complaint About Licensee

UR
H O M E   R E A L T Y

_____ ← Date and address

_____
_____
_____

Dear _____ :

We received your letter dated [June 3]. I was very surprised that a complaint was made to your office about our agent, [Yvonne Spies]. I have set forth the facts in the attachment and have included signed statements from those in our office who are involved.

[Although we believe the complaint is entirely without merit], you can expect our full cooperation in this matter. If you have further questions, please do not hesitate to contact me.

Yours truly,

_____

Enclosures: ← Card, statement of fact, agent statement(s)

General Complaint

UR
HOME REALTY

_____ ← Date and address

_____
_____
_____

Dear _____:

I regret that you have not been satisfied with the [1. services 2. actions] of [UR Home Realty]. Although we don't always succeed, we nevertheless strive in good faith to meet the needs of [both clients and customers]. While unfortunate, this failure will help us to improve our service in the future.

[1. I will be calling you to arrange a meeting so we can satisfactorily resolve the problem. 2. I want you to know that my door is open to you at any time to discuss problems freely, and I would be happy to meet with you at your convenience.]

Yours truly,

_____

Enclosure: ← Card

Offer to Arbitrate/Offer to Meet

UR
H O M E   R E A L T Y

_____ ← Date and address

_____
_____
_____

Dear _____:

[UR Home Realty] would like t o resolve [your complaint] in a fair and equitable manner. [What could be fairer than to submit our disagreement to an impartial arbitrator for binding arbitration? If this appears satisfactory to you, please contact me and we will work out the details of selecting an arbitrator.] [I will call you to arrange a meeting that is convenient to your schedule.]

Yours truly,

_____

Enclosure: ← Card

Note: A face-to-face meeting to reach an agreement would generally be preferred to arbitration, although arbitration is generally preferable to a lawsuit.

Offer to Meet to Resolve Complaint

UR
H O M E   R E A L T Y

_____ ← Date and address

_____
_____
_____

Dear _____:

Based on [1. your letter dated July 13   2. our phone conversation on July 13], it is clear that you feel [UR Home Realty] has not treated you in a fair and proper manner.

While I sincerely believe our actions were at all times fair and professional, I am nevertheless disturbed by your feelings toward us. [We consider ourselves a part of the community, and we want very much to maintain a harmonious relationship with all our neighbors.]

I will contact you in the next few days to arrange a meeting to resolve this problem in a mutually satisfactory manner.

Yours truly,

_____

Enclosure: ← Card

Note: Whenever possible, settlement offers should be made face to face. A meeting is preferable to an offer by letter. It is recommended that an attorney review any settlement offer.

Notification to State Department of Real Estate About Violation of the Law

UR
HOME REALTY

_____ ← Date and address

_____
_____
_____

Dear _____:

I am sorry to report an apparent violation of our state real estate law by [1. one of my associates   2. a licensed real estate agent].

[On April 12, 2012, Timothy Jones, a real estate salesperson licensed under my broker's license, accepted a $5,000 cash deposit from Kermit Pugh. Mr. Jones has not contacted our office since he received the deposit and has not been home in the four days since he accepted the deposit. We therefore assume that Mr. Jones has appropriated the deposit for his own use. We have notified the district attorney of these facts.]

We will fully cooperate with your office in any investigation and will promptly supply any additional information requested.

Yours truly,

_____

Enclosure: ← Card

Note: Failure to promptly notify the state licensing authority of a violation of the law could place the broker's license in jeopardy. Because of the importance of this letter, consider special handling, such as an overnight delivery service requiring a signature upon receipt.

C H A P T E R

PROPERTY MANAGEMENT

Notice to Tenant—New Management

UR
HOME REALTY

_____ ← Date and address

_____
_____
_____

Dear _____:

As of [August 1, U R Home Realty] [1. will take 2. has taken] over the property management of your building at [11476 J Street]. All tenant deposits have been transferred to our firm.

[James Howard in apartment 2A] [1. will remain 2. is your new] resident manager. [He] will be your contact for any problems or suggestions you may have. [Your present lease will be fully honored.]

Rents will be [1. paid to Mr. Howard, with checks made out to Ur Home Realty 2. sent to U R Home Realty at _____]. [A postage-paid envelope is included for your rent.]

If you have any questions, do not hesitate to contact [Mr. Howard], the resident manager, or myself.

Yours truly,

_____

Enclosure: ← Card, self-addressed stamped envelope

No Longer Property Manager

UR
H O M E   R E A L T Y

_____ ← Date and address

_____
_____
_____

Dear _____:

As of [August 1, 2012], UR Home Realty will no longer manage your building at [1114 Elm Street]. The new management is [We Rent Realty]. All leases and deposits have been turned over to them.

All rents and notices should be sent to [We Rent Realty at 1422 Western Avenue, Suite 16].

[Mr. Kim in apartment 3A will remain your resident manager.]

I have enjoyed our past relationship and am certain you will be pleased with the management of [We Rent Realty].

Yours truly,

_____

Enclosure: ← Card

Response to Owner Cancellation of Management Contract

UR
HOME REALTY

_____ ← Date and address

_____
_____
_____

Dear _____:

We have received your [letter dated January 12, 2012,] in which you unilaterally cancelled our management contract for [Westfield Towers at 811 West Morgan Blvd.].

The contract was entered into on [June 1, 2011, at which time the property had a 42 percent office vacancy factor that we were able to reduce to 17 percent by January 1, 2012]. We have worked diligently to meet our contractual obligations.

The contract, which expires [May 31, 2014], provides that we are entitled to [5.5 percent of the gross monthly rents received] for the term of the agreement.

Your cancellation of our agency does not terminate your obligations.

[1. We therefore insist that you make your monthly payment in the amount specified until the end of the contract term.] [2. It would be in our best interests to negotiate a mutually satisfactory settlement. I will be contacting you so that we can resolve this matter.]

Yours truly,

_____

Note: This letter should be sent by registered mail. At times, owners are willing to pay management fees when there are significant problems but are less willing when the problems appear to be solved.

Agreed Cancellation of Property Management Contract

UR
HOME REALTY

_____ ← Date and address

_____
_____
_____

Dear _____:

In [your letter dated August 1], you indicated that you wish to cancel our management contract. While we have strived to serve your best interests, we are sorry that you have not been satisfied with our efforts.

I am enclosing a cancellation agreement. Please sign and return [2] copies. This agreement relieves both you as owner and [UR Home Realty] as property manager of all further liabilities.

I will call you in the next few days in order to arrange to turn over all keys, tenant records, leases, and deposits pending a final accounting and payment of any outstanding obligations.

If UR Home Realty can be of assistance to you again in the future, please contact us.

Yours truly,

_____

Enclosure: ← Card, Cancellation Agreement

Note: There are times when it is not worth asserting your legal right, such as when only a short time remains on the contract or where the financial benefits are negated by problems requiring a great deal of time.

Rental Inquiry

To:

From: agent@urhome.com

Subject: Requested Available Apartments

Attachment(s):   [Apartment Photos/Details]

Dear _____:

In response to your inquiry, we have the following units available for [1. June 1 occupancy   2. immediate occupancy] that appear to meet your stated requirements:

[Two-bedroom, two-bath at 1822 West Stevens, $1,250/month, with $600 security deposit on a one-year lease (no pets).]

[Two-bedroom at 731 West Third Street, $980/month, with a $1,000 security deposit on a one-year lease—small pets allowed.]

[1. You can view available apartments on our Web site, [www.urhome.com], 2. Enclosed are photos and descriptive information.]

I will call you to discuss your real estate needs and to arrange to show you available rental property in [Orchard Ridge]. [We also have several homes and condominiums that can be purchased with very low and even no down payment and with monthly payments within your indicated payment range.]

Yours truly,

Note: E-mail with photos would be the preferred method of written communication. Consider calling your contact to obtain an e-mail address if you don't have one on file.

Approval of Rental Application

To:

From: agent@urhome.com

Subject: Rental Application Approved

Dear _____:

Congratulations!

Your rental application has been approved for [733 West Third Street] with occupancy on [November 1].

Please come to [our office] by [October 20] to sign the [one-year] lease and to pay the balance of the required deposits as follows:

[Rent November 1–30]	[$1,150]
[Last month's rent]	[$1,150]
[Security deposit]	[$500]
Total advance rent and deposits	[$2,800]
[Less application deposit]	[($200)]
Balance due:	[$2,600]

I look forward to seeing you.

Yours truly,

_____

Rental Application Rejection #1

To:

From: agent@urhome.com

Subject: Your Rental Application

Dear _____:

I have mailed you [1. your check 2. our check] in the amount of [$175], which constitutes the return of your rental application deposit for [4312 Waverly Way] [less the nonrefundable credit report fee of ($25)].

Another applicant for the premises has been accepted.

[We do have several other units available in other buildings:]

Address	Size	Rental
[1732 Third Street	2 BR, 2 bath	$925]
[501 Chestnut Circle	2 BR, 1 ½ bath	$875]
[2001 Jupiter Avenue	2 BR, 1 bath	$790]

[1. If you wish to view any of these units, please contact our office. 2. I will call you to arrange to show you any of our offerings that interest you. 3. You can view these apartments on our Web site, (www.urhome.com).]

[We also have a number of properties for sale with (1. reasonable 2. low) down payments. If you would like more information on these, please contact me.] The services of [UR Home Realty] are at your disposal to secure suitable housing for your family.

Yours truly,

_____

Note: By mentioning other housing opportunities, and that you will continue to help, you lessen the likelihood that rental applicants will feel discriminated against. Of course, if the reason for rejection of the tenant was poor credit or rental history, you would not want to mention other properties. (See the next e-mail.)

Rental Application Rejection #2

To:

From: agent@urhome.com

Subject: Your Rental Application

Dear _____:

We regret to inform you that your rental application for [2001 Jupiter Avenue] has been rejected. [The apartment has been rented to another applicant.]

We have mailed you [1. your check   2. our check] for [$300], which represents the return of your rental deposit [less the nonrefundable credit report fee of ($20) as agreed to in your rental application].

If you have any questions, please contact me.

Yours truly,

_____

Note: We strongly suggest that you avoid listing reasons for rejecting applications in your letter because they tend to lead to protracted confrontations. You should fully document your files, however, because applicants sometimes claim wrongful bias. If you rented the unit to another applicant, the file should support the choice made.

Late Payment—Waiver of Late Charge

To:

CC: [Property manager]

From: agent@urhome.com

Subject: Payment received late

Dear _____:

Your rent payment for the month of [October 2012] was due at our office no later than [October 10, 2012]. However, we did not receive it until [October 14, 2012].

A late charge of [$50] is authorized by paragraph [6] of your lease.

[Because this is your first late payment,] we will waive the late charge in this instance. However, it is essential that future rent payments be received on time. If any future rent payment is received late, a late charge will be assessed against you as provided by your lease agreement.

Yours truly,

_____

Late Payment Charge

To:

CC: [Resident manager]

From: agent@urhome.com

Subject: Late payment charge

Dear _____:

Your rent payment for [October] was due at our office on [Octobe- 10]. It was not received until [October 21].

You are hereby notified that in accord with paragraph [4] of your lease, you have been assessed a late charge of [$50].

Please remit this amount immediately.

Yours truly,

_____

Bad Check

UR
HOME REALTY

_____ ← Date and address

_____
_____
_____

Dear _____ :

Your check number [5811] in the amount of [$1,100] made out to [UR Home Realty] for the [April] rent of [apartment 2700 at 4914 Highland Avenue] has been returned to us from your bank marked insufficient funds.

Please see that this office is furnished with cash, a money order, or a cashier's check in the amount of [$1,150] by [April 20]. [This amount includes a charge of ($25) for the returned check, under the terms of your lease, as well as a late charge of ($25).] Failure to comply will be regarded as a breach of your legal obligations.

[All future rent payments must be in cash, a cashier's check, or a money order].

Yours truly,

_____

Enclosure: ← Card

cc: [Resident manager]

Note: No threat of legal action is made, although it might possibly be inferred. A date is set to express urgency. The letter makes clear that a personal check will not be accepted. Personal delivery of this letter is preferred but, if you mail it, consider using registered mail that requires a signature upon receipt or an overnight delivery service.

Rent Increase #1

UR
HOME REALTY

_____ ← Date and address

_____
_____
_____

Dear _____:

Because of [1. increased expenses 2. increased interest rates 3. improvements we have made], a rental adjustment has become necessary.

As of [May 1], the rent for [5800 Crescent Cove, #3-S] will be increased from the current [$870] per month to [$910] per month [—a 4.6 percent increase].

Yours truly,

_____

Enclosure: ← Card

cc: [Resident property manager]

Note: Be certain that notices comply with your state laws as to content, notice period, and service of the notice (registered mail might be required). Showing the dollar rent increase as a small percentage of the total rent tends to minimize the increase.

Rent Increase #2

UR
HOME REALTY

_____ ← Date and address

_____
_____
_____

Dear _____:

You are hereby notified, in accordance with [Arizona] law, that as of [January 1, 2013], your rent will be increased from [$875] per month to [$925] per month for the premises at [643 Jupiter Lane, second floor].

Yours truly,

_____

Enclosure: ← Card

cc: [Resident property manager]

Note: Make certain that rent increase notices are given for the statutory period. For example, a number of states require that notification be given at least 30 days before the rent increase; in some cases, it is 60 days. In some states, the notification period must end on the day rent is due. Consider using registered or certified mail, and request return receipts. This avoids any claim of nondelivery or of your notice being mistaken for an advertisement. Your state statutes may specify the manner of delivering the notice as well as the form of the notice. If maintenance work, such as redecorating common areas, is scheduled before a rent increase, tenants are less likely to be antagonistic to the increase.

Notice to Cease Prohibited Activity/Breach of Rules

UR
H O M E   R E A L T Y

_____ ← Date and address

_____
_____
_____

Dear _____:

It has come to our attention that [you have been performing major automobile repair work in your parking space at 110 Stardust Lane].

This is a violation of [1. your lease 2. the occupancy rules and regulations you signed at the time of rental].

You are hereby ordered to cease this activity immediately, or corrective action will be required in accord with your lease.

Yours truly,

_____

Enclosure: ← Card

cc: [Resident property manager]

Note: Normally, the resident manager should handle this matter.

Resident Manager—Problems

To:

From: agent@urhome.com

Subject: Property Deficiencies

Dear _____:

[1. An inspection of the property at (1295 Plymouth Circle) revealed the following (1. deficiency 2. deficiencies): 2. We have received a complaint regarding the following:]

■ [Sprinklers are spraying into the street.]

■ [The garbage container is often left open, attracting flies.]

■ [Three exterior lights are inoperative.]

Please rectify the [1. problem(s) 2. deficiency 3. deficiencies] [1. as soon as practical 2. immediately] and notify me as to the action taken.

If you have any questions, please contact me.

Yours truly,

_____

Note: A phone or an e-mail notification is preferable to a letter because of letter delays.

Notice to Tenant—Failure to Maintain Exterior or Lawn

UR
H O M E   R E A L T Y

_____ ← Date and address

_____
_____
_____

Dear _____:

In [1. driving by 2. inspecting] the [home at 12 West Davis Street], which you are renting from our office, I was surprised to see that [the lawn has not been cared for].

Under the terms of your lease, you are required to [maintain the landscaping]. Unless [the lawn is properly maintained by August 1], we will have to contract for the work with [a gardening service] and add the charges to your rent.

Yours truly,

_____

Enclosure: ← Card

Notice of Lease Automatic Renewal

UR
H O M E   R E A L T Y

_____ ← Date and address

_____
_____
_____

Dear _____:

Your present lease for [the two-bedroom house] at [660 Stardust Circle] expires on [January 1, 2013].

This is to remind you that unless you give notice to the contrary by [December 1, 2012], the lease by its terms will be automatically extended for [another year]. If you have any questions, please contact me.

Yours truly,

_____

Enclosure: ← Card

cc: [Resident property manager]

Note: Although many owners don't remind tenants of the automatic renewal, the reminder does avoid future problems. In some states, automatic renewal cannot be enforced.

Lease Expiration Notice—New Lease

UR
_____
H O M E   R E A L T Y

_____ ← Date and address

_____
_____
_____

Dear _____:

Your lease for [660 Maple Lane] expires on [September 1, 2012]. I have enclosed a new lease for the premises, which is substantially the same as your old lease [1. at the same rent 2. except that the rent has been increased to ($1,400). The higher rent is required because of cost increases in the operation and management of the property].

Please sign and return [two] copies of the new lease to my office by [July 15, 2012]. If I do not receive your new lease by this date, I will assume that you do not wish to remain in possession and we will seek a new tenant.

Yours truly,

_____

Enclosures: ← Card, lease

cc: [Resident apartment manager]

Note: Although providing reasons for rent increases is not necessary, your action will seem less arbitrary and help to maintain better tenant relations. Rather than mailing the letter and the lease, a better approach would be for the apartment manager to hand-deliver it to the tenant.

Tenant Notice of Leaving in Violation of Lease

UR
H O M E   R E A L T Y

_____ ← Date and address

_____
_____
_____

Dear _____:

Your current lease, dated [January 1, 2012], does not expire until [January 1, 2013]. If you wish to vacate the premises before this date, you will be held liable for the cost of rerenting the premises, as well as for any rental loss incurred.

If you wish to locate a tenant to assume your lease obligations, we will allow a lease assignment subject to our approval based on our reasonable rental criteria. You, of course, would remain liable if the new tenant defaults on the lease.

Please contact me immediately about your intentions. If you are vacating on [September 1, as you indicated], I want to begin immediately to find a new tenant in order to keep your legal obligations to a minimum.

Yours truly,

_____

Enclosure: ← Card

cc: [Resident apartment manager]

Note: This notice should be sent by registered mail or an overnight delivery service to emphasize its importance.

Tenant Vacated in Violation of Lease

UR
H O M E   R E A L T Y

_____ ← Date and address

_____
_____
_____

Dear _____:

I have been informed that on [April 15] you vacated the premises at [1700 Sycamore Avenue]. [1. Your lease required a 30-day notice, which was not given. 2. Your lease does not expire until (June 1).] Therefore, you will be held liable [1. for the rental until the end of the lease period 2. for the 30-day notice period expiring (May 15)].

[If we are able to rerent the premises before the above date, your liability will be reduced by the rent received for said period less the costs of rerenting the premises.]

[You are also being charged with cleaning, repair, and trash removal costs of ($280). An itemized list is attached.]

Please contact this office immediately to make arrangements for fulfilling your obligation.

Yours truly,

_____

Enclosure: ← Card, [cleaning and repair expenses]

cc: [Resident apartment manager]

Note: This letter might require modification based on state law. Contact legal counsel.

Notice to Vacate

UR
HOME REALTY

_____ ← Date and address

_____
_____
_____

Dear _____:

In accordance with [1. the terms of your tenancy 2. (Arizona) law], you are hereby notified that you are ordered to vacate the premises at [6603 Sycamore Parkway] by [May 1, 2012]. This notice satisfies the [30-day notice] required by [state law].

Agent for: [UR Home Management]

_____

Enclosure: ← Card

cc: [Resident manager]

Note: Be certain that your notice and the service of the notice conform with your state law (legal forms can be used in lieu of a letter). Registered mail or personal service might be required. You may have to post the notice on the door to the premises. In some states, the notification period must end on the day rent is due. Check with an attorney, and then modify the notice if required.

Acknowledgment of Tenant's Notice to Vacate

UR

H O M E   R E A L T Y

_____ ← Date and address

_____
_____
_____

Dear _____:

We acknowledge your notice to vacate the premises at [3120 West Lincoln, Unit 8] by [March 1, 2012].

You will be called by [1. the manager, (Mr. Jones), 2. this office] to arrange to show your [apartment] to prospective renters. We will try to give you as much notice as possible.

[Mr. Jones], the [resident manager], will conduct an inspection of the unit when you have vacated. You may wish to be present at this inspection. Within [14 days] of the inspection, your property damage bond will be returned to you, less any rent that may be due and damage other than normal wear and tear.

If you have any questions or desire help in locating housing, please contact us.

Yours truly,

_____

Enclosure: ← Card

cc: [Resident property manager]

Tenant Letter—End-of-Lease Inspection

UR
H O M E   R E A L T Y

_____ ← Date and address

_____
_____
_____

Dear _____:

In accord with [1. your notice 2. our notice 3. the rental agreement], you will be vacating the premises at [1140 Hercules Court, Unit 8B] on [April 30].

We will conduct an inspection of the premises at [2:00 PM] on [April 30] to determine whether there is any damage to the premises other than normal wear and tear [and whether any items are missing from the premises]. [1. After this inspection 2. Within (14) days of this inspection], your security deposit will be returned to you, minus deductions for any damage to the premises other than normal wear and tear [or for any missing items].

If you wish, you may be present for this inspection.

Yours truly,

_____

Enclosure: ← Card

cc: [Resident manager]

Note: This letter reminds tenants that they should leave the premises in good condition, and it will probably reduce the cleaning requirements before rerenting.

Notice to Tenant of Damage on Vacating Premises

UR
HOME REALTY

_____ ← Date and address

_____
_____
_____

Dear _____ :

Inspection of the premises at [6603 Sycamore, third floor,] that you vacated on [April 1] revealed that [1. the living room floor is badly scratched in several places 2. the ceiling fan and the miniblinds from the dining room are missing 3. the bathroom mirror is broken].

Because the [1. damages 2. missing articles] are not normal wear and tear, we have made the necessary [1. repairs 2. replacements] and have deducted the cost of [$325] from your [security deposit]. [The balance of ($75) is enclosed.]

[Because the cost of (1. repairs 2. replacements), ($500), exceeds the amount of your property damage bond, please remit ($300) to this office no later than (4:00 PM) on (April 10).]

[The necessary (1. repairs 2. replacements) have resulted in costs of ($300). Please remit this amount to our office no later than (4:00 PM) on (April 10).]

Yours truly,

_____

Enclosures: ← Card, property damage bond statement

cc: [Resident manager]

Note: When a definite date for the alternative paragraphs is provided, the former tenant will assume that legal action will be taken if the remittance is not paid by this date, although no threat is being made. An overnight delivery service should be considered for this letter.

Tenant Complaint—Forwarded for Action

To:

CC: [Resident manager]

From: agent@urhome.com

Subject: Problem to Be Resolved Soon

Dear _____:

I have received your [letter] about [unauthorized parking in your space].

I have forwarded your concerns to [the resident manager], who will be contacting you directly.

I sincerely hope that the problem is resolved to your satisfaction. If you have any other questions, call the manager or me.

Yours truly,

_____

Tenant Complaint—Action Taken

To:

CC: [Mr. Brown]

From: agent@urhome.com

Subject: Problem Resolved

Attachment(s):   Card

Dear _____:

I have received your [letter] about [unauthorized parking in your space].

[The offending party has been contacted], and we hope that the [problem has been resolved]. If the problem continues, please contact [1. me directly 2. (Mr. Brown), the building manager].

Yours truly,

_____

Tenant Complaint—No Action Taken

To:

CC: [Building manager]

From: agent@urhome.com

Subject: [Tenant Complaint]

Dear _____:

I have received your complaint [that the neighbor's children have been disturbing you]. [Because we do not discriminate as to families, the noise of children playing must be expected, although it can be exasperating at times.]

[1. Because we are unable to solve your problem, we would be willing to allow you to break your lease upon (30) days' notice. Please let me know what you decide. 2. When your lease expires, we would be happy to help you find a unit that better meets your requirements.]

Yours truly,

_____

Note: If there is a waiting list for units and the tenant has been an irritant to management, offering to allow the tenant out of the lease might be in your best interests.

Notice to Tenant of Lessor Entry

UR
H O M E   R E A L T Y

_____ ← Date and address

_____
_____
_____

Dear _____:

In accord with the terms of your lease, we will [1. make an inspection of the premises 2. show the premises to a prospective buyer 3. repair the kitchen floor in your unit] at [9:00 AM] on [Tuesday, February 6].

If you are unable to be present at that time, please contact [1. this office 2. Mr. Brown, the building manager] [1. so that a more convenient time can be arranged 2. to make certain that the building manager has all necessary keys].

Yours truly,

_____

Enclosure: ← Card

cc: [Building manager]

Note: A phone call or a personal visit by the resident manager would be the preferable way to inform the tenant.

i

Notice of Work on Premises

UR
HOME REALTY

_____ ← Date and address

_____
_____
_____

Dear _____:

In the next [1. few days   2. few weeks], we will be [1. painting the lobby   2. replacing the air conditioning]. We hope that you will not be inconvenienced by the work, which will be confined to normal working hours.

[Access to your apartment will be required on (April 15). If you are not home, our resident manager, (Jane Smith), will remain in your unit while workers are present. (Please provide keys to the manager, if required.)]

Yours truly,

_____

Enclosure: ← Card

cc: [Resident manager]

Note: This letter serves another purpose in that it informs the tenants they are getting something for their rent; the owner is putting money back into the building. This service makes a subsequent rent increase more palatable to the tenants.

Confirmation of Telephone Work Order

To:

CC: [Building manager]

From: agent@urhome.com

Subject: Work Order Confirmation

Dear _____:

This will confirm our agreement on [May 10] for you to [provide a pest control inspection] at [6501 Crescent Circle]. It is understood that the work must be completed by [June 1].

[Please call our office 24 hours before you begin work so we can be certain someone will be present to provide access to the property.]

We acknowledge that your charge for said work shall be [$125].

[Work order number (1073) has been assigned to this project. Please reference said work order in any billing or other correspondence.]

[Bill (1. this office 2. Mr. and Mrs. James) for the work no later than (July 1).]

Yours truly,

Request for Bids

UR
H O M E   R E A L T Y

_____ ← Date and address

_____
_____
_____

Dear _____ :

We would appreciate your bid for [replacement of the roof] for the [48-unit building] at [1146 Washington Place].

Work must be performed in accordance with the attached specifications.

Please submit your bid by April 15.

Yours truly,

_____

Enclosure: ← Card, Specifications

cc: [Building manager]

Note: Bond requirements, if any, as well as insurance coverage, indemnity for injury, damages, etc., should be part of your work specifications form. In some instances, professional help should be obtained for work specifications.

Repair Request to Owner—Authorization Required

UR

H O M E   R E A L T Y

_____ ← Date and address

_____
_____
_____

Dear _____:

Your property at [74181 Lexington Avenue] requires the following repairs:

[Exterior lighting needs to be replaced to comply with code requirements.]

[The condenser unit for apartment 2C's air conditioner must be replaced.]

Based on the enclosed [1. estimate 2. bid], [1. the cost for this work will be ($1,470) 2. the cost for this work is likely to exceed ($1,000)].

Our management contract requires your authorization for any repair that exceeds [$1,000]. We therefore request your authorization to make the required repairs. Failure to authorize repairs could result in [1. vacancies and loss of income 2. damage to the property 3. being cited for code violations].

Your prompt attention to this matter would be appreciated.

Yours truly,

_____

Enclosures: ← Card, bid or estimate [photos]

cc: [Resident manager]

Note: If a photo of the problem would help emphasize the necessity of the work, consider enclosing a photo.

BROKER, LENDER, AND ATTORNEY LETTERS

Welcome to New Broker

UR

H O M E   R E A L T Y

_____ ← Date and address

_____
_____
_____

Dear _____:

As a fellow [1. real estate broker   2. REALTOR®], I would like to welcome you to [the growing West Side].

I am certain that we will have many productive dealings in the coming years because cooperation is the basis of real estate success. [I will stop by to meet you personally in a few weeks after you are settled.]

I wish you success in your new office—welcome!

Sincerely,

_____

Enclosure: ← Card

MLS Caravan—Breakfast or Lunch

To:

From: agent@urhome.com

Subject: Caravan—[October 28], [Refreshments]

Be sure to visit [37 West Toliver Avenue] and be my guest for

[1. Continental breakfast

2. Breakfast buffet

3. Very special brunch

4. Luncheon buffet

5. Coffee and bagels]

During the [MLS] caravan on [Tuesday]

[October 28,] from [9:00 AM to 11:00 AM]; [click here to view]

[Agent]

[UR Home Realty]

Note: In areas where there are more listings than agents can possibly visit, you may need something extra to bring in agents. Food acts as a magnet in these situations. Set up the e-mail with links so the recipient can click on the address (or other item) to view photos, take a virtual tour, or obtain property details.

Invitation—Agent Open House

To:	
From:	agent@urhome.com
Subject:	Agent Open House—[Food/Drink]

YOU ARE INVITED

To a very special agent-only

OPEN HOUSE

at

[72426 Rodeo Avenue]

[View Property]

From [4:00 to 7:00 PM]

[Friday, April 3]

[Cocktails and Hors d'oeuvres]

[Buffet Dinner/Refreshments]

[Drawing for Valuable Door Prizes

3 Electronic Tape Measures to Be Given Away]

RSVP

[UR Home Realty]

[John Jones 602-555-8200]

[jjones@urhome.com]

Note: An RSVP will usually increase attendance because it makes the invitation more special to the recipients, and once they have responded, they are more likely to actually come.

Office Open House Invitation

H O M E   R E A L T Y

Open House

[922 West Broadway]

[Wednesday, April 5]

[5:00 to 8:00 PM]

Come visit us at our [1. new office   2. new branch office].

Refreshments will be served!

Note: This invitation can be sent to owners, investors, escrow and title companies, and lenders, as well as other brokers and salespeople. You could have this invitation printed on regular invitation stock or send by e-mail.

Holiday Open House Invitation

H O M E   R E A L T Y

Cordially Invites You to Our Holiday Season Open House

[922 West 52nd Street]

[Friday, December 23]

[5:00 to 7:00 PM]

Please Visit Us

Refreshments will be served.

[Sprig of holly here]

Note: Invitations should be on regular invitation card stock. Send to lenders, investors, owners, and so on. Send as an e-mail to broker and salesperson members of your MLS. Small wrapped gifts with names of agents who participated in transactions could be placed under a Christmas tree. (Before giving any gift to an agent, obtain the permission of the agent's broker to do so.)

Wanted: [Palm Springs] Referrals

To:
From: agent@urhome.com
Subject: Profit from Palm Springs referrals
Attachment(s): [Resume]

Dear _____:

Do you want your [Palm Springs] referral to result in sales and commission checks?

I have a proven track record of success with referral clients. Please check my attached resume.

Sincerely,

_____

Broker Referral Thank You

UR
H O M E   R E A L T Y

_____ ← Date and address

_____
_____
_____

Dear _____:

Thank you very much for referring [Jane Smith] to this office.

I have shown [the Smiths] a number of properties, [and I am confident I will be able to meet their housing needs].

[I hope I will be sending you a check within a short time.]

If I can ever be of service to you, don't hesitate to call me.

Yours truly,

_____

Enclosure: ← Card

Broker Referral Thank You—No Sale

UR

HOME REALTY

_____ ← Date and address

_____

_____

_____

Dear _____:

Thank you very much for referring [Joseph Jones] to our office. Although we contacted [the Joneses] promptly [and showed them a number of homes], we regret that we were unsuccessful in providing for their home purchase.

I want you to know that our failure was not the result of lack of effort. In fact, if there is another opportunity, I would like to show you that [UR Home Realty] does make sales and is worthy of your referrals.

Yours truly,

_____

Enclosure: ← Card

Broker Referral—Notice Of Sale

UR
H O M E   R E A L T Y

_____ ← Date and address

_____
_____
_____

Dear _____:

Just a note to let you know that [Sylvia Smith], whom you referred to us, has [purchased a home through this office]. The closing is scheduled for [June 1]. On closing, we will immediately forward your referral fee of [$4,802] based on our office commission of [$24,010].

We appreciate the referral and look forward to future cooperation with your office.

Yours truly,

_____

Enclosure: ← Card

Referral Fee—Transmittal

UR

HOME REALTY

_____ ← Date and address

_____
_____
_____

Dear _____ :

Enclosed is our check in the amount of [$4,802] for your referral of [John Jones], as well as our commission statement. Thank you again for recommending [UR Home Realty].

We look forward to working with you in the future.

Yours truly,

_____

Enclosures: ← Card, check, commission statement

Note: We suggest that checks be sent by FedEx, priority mail, or similar special delivery service.

Seeking an Investment Property

To:

From: agent@urhome.com

Subject: Seeking Investment Property

Dear _____:

I am working with a prospective investor who has [more than $500,000] to invest and desires [1. residential property 2. income property 3. a raw-land investment]. My buyer's primary objective is [1. appreciation 2. income 3. tax-sheltered income]. [Of course, safety is also a consideration.]

My investor [1. wants a positive cash flow 2. will accept a negative cash flow 3. wants at least a break-even cash flow] with an [1. all-cash 2. moderately leveraged 3. highly leveraged] investment.

If you have any investment property listed with your office that you believe would interest my buyer, I would very much like to work with you.

Yours truly,

_____

Note: Send as an e-mail.

Request for Commission

UR

HOME REALTY

_____ ← Date and address

_____
_____
_____

Dear _____:

[On the morning of October 12, Jean Jacobs of our office showed a home that you had listed at 1112 Kings Drive to William and Tiffany Apple. That afternoon, you held an open house at the same property, and the Apples stopped at the house. They have indicated that they told your salesperson, Jim Peters, that they had seen the house that morning with Mrs. Jacobs. Mr. Peters proceeded to prepare a purchase agreement, which the Apples signed and the owner accepted.] These facts clearly indicate that [UR Home Realty] was the procuring cause for the sale and is therefore entitled to the sales commission.

I will be calling you to arrange a meeting so this matter can be resolved.

Yours truly,

_____

Enclosure: ← Card

Note: An attempt to resolve a problem such as this should preferably be made in person. If unresolved, arbitration should be sought.

Broker Commission Split—Transmittal

UR
H O M E   R E A L T Y

_____ ← Date and address

_____
_____
_____

Dear _____:

Enclosed is our check for [$11,850], which represents [50] percent of the total commission for [your sale] of the property located at [5 Sycamore Circle] to [Janet Smith].

I have enclosed a copy of the closing statement for your records.

Your cooperation was greatly appreciated, and I look forward to sending you many more commissions.

Yours truly,

_____

Enclosures: ← Card, check, closing statement

Note: Consider special treatment for check transmittal by sending it FedEx or in a similar manner.

Breach of Procedure by Our Office

UR

H O M E   R E A L T Y

_____ ← Date and address

_____
_____
_____

Dear _____:

I want to apologize personally to you for an unfortunate breach of procedure by our office. [1. On June 16, one of our salespeople contacted one of your owners, Janet Smith, without going through your office. 2. One of our salespeople contacted James Smith, whose listing was in full effect with your office, about obtaining a listing.] The reasons for the breach and the fact that at the time the salesperson did not realize that [1. he 2. she] was in breach of ethics does not matter.

What does matter is that one of my salespeople failed to respect your rights. I have already discussed the situation with my salesperson. I will do everything in my power to make certain that such an action is not repeated.

Yours truly,

_____

Enclosure: ← Card

Breach of Procedure by Your Office

UR

H O M E   R E A L T Y

_____ ← Date and address

_____
_____
_____

Dear _____:

I am sorry to have to inform you that on [August 21], your salesperson, [Sylvia Smith], [contacted James Smith, whose listing was in full effect with our office, about obtaining a listing. Our office For Sale sign was on the front lawn].

This type of action cannot be condoned because, in our profession, cooperation is the basis of success. We hope that such action is not repeated in the future.

Yours truly,

_____

Enclosure: ← Card

Arbitration Notice

_____

UR
H O M E   R E A L T Y

_____ ← Date and address

_____

_____

_____

Dear _____:

Based on your failure to pay [UR Home Realty the selling commission for the sale of 1112 Kings Drive to William and Liz Apple], we are requesting arbitration [of this matter with the San Marco Board of REALTORS® in accord with board rules and regulations].

Yours truly,

_____

Enclosure: ← Card

_____

Note: Binding arbitration is possible when both parties are members of an organization that requires arbitration.

Loan Application Transmittal

UR
H O M E   R E A L T Y

_____ ← Date and address

_____

_____

_____

Dear _____ :

Enclosed you will find the completed loan application of [John and Mary Brown] for the purchase of a home located at [65 Jupiter Lane].

If you have any problems whatsoever or desire any additional information, please contact me [or Meg Smith].

Yours truly,

_____

Enclosures: ← Card, loan application

cc: [John and Mary Brown]

Note: We suggest sending loan packages by overnight delivery services, such as FedEx, when it cannot be delivered in person or when an online application is not possible.

Request to Lender to Expedite Loan Request

UR

H O M E   R E A L T Y

_____ ← Date and address

_____
_____
_____

Dear _____ :

[Mr. and Mrs. Smith] recently applied for a loan through your office for the purchase of the home at [111 Stardust Circle].

Because of unusual needs of the [1. seller   2. buyer], it is necessary that this sale be closed by [August 1, 2012]. Although I realize that this places a strain on your office, I would nevertheless greatly appreciate any efforts you can provide to expedite this transaction.

Yours truly,

_____

Enclosure: ← Card

cc: [Mr. and Mrs. Smith]

Note: A better approach would be a phone call to the loan officer and monitoring the status of the loan by phone or e-mail.

To Lender—Low Appraisal

To:	
CC:	[1. Buyer 2. Seller]
From:	agent@urhome.com
Subject:	Re: Appraisal for [1121 Hummingbird Circle]
Attachment(s):	Comparative Market Analysis

Dear _____:

I was surprised by the appraisal made on [April 3] for the property at [1121 Hummingbird Circle] for [Mr. and Mrs. Jones's] loan application.

The appraisal of [$260,000] does not appear to reflect recent sales of comparable property in the area. [(Three) recent sales were omitted from your appraisal.]

I have attached a comparative market analysis based on all the sales in [the Orchard Ridge subdivision] within the past [90 days]. You will see from comparable sales that your appraisal, as stated, appears to be at least [$60,000] under current market value.

I would appreciate a review of the appraisal.

I have enjoyed our mutually beneficial relationship in the past and hope to continue working with you in the future to arrange the financing for our real estate purchasers.

Yours truly,

_____

Note: In addition to this e-mail, consider a phone call to or personal contact with the loan officer.

Short Sale—Lender Preapproval Sought

UR
_____ HOME REALTY _____

_____ ← Date and address

_____
_____
_____

RE: Loan No: _____

Dear _____: [Loan Mitigation Officer]

Our firm has recently listed the home at [123 Midland Boulevard in Fayetteville, Michigan,] for sale. The owners [John and Kristen Thomas] are currently in default on a mortgage with your [bank]. The balance on the loan is [$242,522]. Because of changes in circumstances, the Thomas family can be expected to fall further in arrears. [The house is currently vacant.]

The value of the property has declined significantly so that it is now worth less than the balance owing on the mortgage. I would like your concurrence in offering the property as a short sale at a price of [$211,000] with the understanding that any offer would be subject to a final lender approval.

I believe that the enclosed documentation will justify this request. I have enclosed the following:

- Hardship letter from Mr. and Mrs. Thomas

- Financial statement showing assets and liabilities of Mr. and Mrs. Thomas

- Copy of bank statements [checking and savings] for the last three months

- Credit card statements for the last three months

- Comparative market analysis prepared by our firm showing all sales in [Shady Acres subdivision] for the last [three] months and estimated present fair market value

- Estimated lender's net based on list price

- Copy of our sale listing

(1)

(2)

I believe you will concur that accepting sale proceeds as fulfillment of the mortgage debt obligation will be in your best interests and that a short sale should be sought.

I will be contacting you to answer any questions you may have.

Yours truly,

_____

Note: Phone calls to the lender should reveal the name of the loan mitigation officer who handles short sales. The benefit of this letter is that prior knowledge should reduce the time for short sale approval as well as reveal whether a short sale is even possible. If there is private mortgage insurance, the lender might prefer to foreclose and go to the insurer for loss suffered. Hardship letters from the owner should show a true hardship problem such as loss of or reduced income, job relocation, or unusual necessary expenses such as medical bills. If the homeowner is not in default and there is not a legitimate hardship, lender approval for a short sale is not likely. Follow this letter with a phone call.

Short Sale Offer—Request for Lender Approval

UR
HOME REALTY

_____ ← Date and address

_____
_____
_____

RE: Loan No: _____

Dear _____: [Loan Mitigation Officer]

Enclose is a purchase offer for [123 Midland Boulevard in Fayetteville, Michigan]. The owners [John and Kristen Thomas] have accepted this offer, subject to your agreement to accept the proceeds of the sale as satisfaction of subject loan.

Based on the attached documentation, I believe you will agree that concurrence of this short sale will be in your [bank's] best interest.

I will be contacting you to answer any questions you may have.

Yours truly,

_____

Attachments:

- Accepted purchase offer

- Loan approved letter for the purchaser's lender

- Hardship letter from Mr. and Mrs. Thomas

- Financial statement [Mr. and Mrs. Thomas]

- Copy of bank statements for the last three months

- Credit card statements for last three months

- Comparative market analysis showing all sales in [Shady Acres subdivision] for the last [three] months and our supported estimate of a value of [$211,000]

- Estimated lender's net after all sale expenses

Note: The fact that a loan has been approved can be a significant factor in obtaining lender approval of the short sale.

Request for Abstract Update

UR
H O M E   R E A L T Y

_____ ← Date and address

_____

_____

_____

Dear _____:

Please update the enclosed abstract of title for the following described property: [insert legal description of property].

Please bill [the seller, Thomas Pike,] for this service.

Yours truly,

_____

Enclosure: ← Card, abstract

cc: [Names of buyer and/or seller]

Note: The abstract should normally be delivered personally. If it is mailed or sent by messenger, obtain a receipt as proof of its delivery. If an escrow agent is used, the escrow agent will handle updating of the abstract. While abstracts are still used in some localities, they have largely been replaced by title insurance.

Request for Attorney Title Opinion

UR
H O M E   R E A L T Y

_____ ← Date and address

_____

_____

_____

Dear _____:

Please provide a title opinion for [Thomas and Cynthia Wooley] for the purchase of [legal description of property].

The updated abstract is enclosed.

Please send the opinion and the abstract to [my office]. Your invoice should be made out to [Mr. and Mrs. Wooley but sent to me].

Yours truly,

_____

Enclosures: ← Card, abstract

cc: [Thomas and Cynthia Wooley]

Note: Generally, abstracts should be hand-delivered to the attorney's office and a receipt should be obtained. In most of the country, title opinions have been replaced by title insurance.

Request for Title Insurance Quote

To:

From: agent@urhome.com

Subject: Title Insurance Quote

Dear _____:

Please provide a title insurance quote for a [standard owners' policy] of title insurance for [1324 Stoneridge Avenue, Fayetteville, Michigan,] in the amount of [$231,000]. The loan amount is [$231,000]. The buyers are [Thomas and Sara Wooley], and the sellers are [James and Heather McKinney].

The property is a [single-family residence].

Yours truly,

_____

Thank You to Loan Officer #1

UR
HOME REALTY

_____ ← Date and address

_____
_____
_____

Dear _____:

I would like to personally thank you for your help in arranging the financing for [Sherman and Joyce Mack] for their recent purchase of the home at [72 Lynn Court].

You not only delivered the loan in a timely manner, but you provided counseling service as well, which was greatly appreciated. You turned what is usually a difficult process for a buyer into a pleasant experience. I hope to work with you and your firm on many future loans.

Yours truly,

_____

Enclosure: ← Card

cc: [Jane Smith, president, ABO Savings Association]

Note: A letter such as this, with copies sent to the president of the bank or the loan broker, will be appreciated by the loan officer. You can expect this loan officer to treat any future loan problems as a priority item.

Thank You to Loan Officer #2

UR
H O M E   R E A L T Y

_____ ← Date and address

_____
_____
_____

Dear _____:

I want to thank you personally for your Herculean efforts, which resulted in our closing the [James C. Smith] loan by [August 1].

Your attention to detail and your honest, straightforward approach proved that what others said couldn't be done can be accomplished with a positive can-do attitude. Working with you was a pleasure, and I look forward to many further transactions with your firm.

Yours truly,

_____

Enclosure: ← Card

cc: [John Jones, president, ABC Savings Association]

Note: This letter and its copy will give you a future ally in the lender's office.

Request for List of REOs

UR

H O M E   R E A L T Y

_____ ← Date and address

_____
_____
_____

Dear _____:

Please provide a list of your present repossessions and give the following information:

- Address and size
- Price and terms (if applicable)
- Obtaining keys for showings (Is a master key available?)

Yours truly,

_____

Enclosure: ← Card

Note: REO is the trade acronym for real estate owned by the lender that is acquired through foreclosure. Make a phone call to identify the officer charged with the disposition of foreclosed properties. If the foreclosures are listed by an agent, you should find out who has the listings. Even though lenders do not want to inventory foreclosed property, some lenders will resist your attempts to help them.

Purchase Contract for Buyer's/Seller's Attorney Approval

UR
H O M E   R E A L T Y

_____ ← Date and address

_____
_____
_____

Dear _____:

Enclosed is the completed purchase contract for the [1. sale by 2. purchase by] your clients [Jim and Jane Schmidt] of [111 Crescent Cove]. If, after your review, you determine that the agreement is legally sufficient, please have [the Schmidts] sign and return [three] copies to this office.

Yours truly,

_____

Enclosure: ← Card, purchase contract

cc: [Jim and Jane Schmidt]

Note: Don't mention changes or modifications. Most attorneys will do so without your reminder. While attorneys are experts on legal sufficiency, they will often go beyond legal sufficiency and suggest a lower price or more advantageous terms for their clients. We suggest hand-delivering this to the attorney's office.

Thank-You Letter to Attorney

UR
H O M E   R E A L T Y

_____ ← Date and address

_____
_____
_____

Dear _____:

Working with you on the [Smiths'] [1. sale 2. purchase] was a pleasure. Your professional and helpful manner made what can sometimes be confrontational a friendly and beneficial transaction.

If I am ever asked to recommend a real estate attorney, I will not hesitate to provide your name.

Yours truly,

_____

Enclosure: ← Card

Note: A thank-you letter such as this will help you to deal with the attorney in a more relaxed manner in the future.

Request for Escrow Fee and Cost Schedules

UR
H O M E   R E A L T Y

_____ ← Date and address

_____
_____
_____

Dear _____:

Please supply me with your current escrow fee schedule, as well as your schedule of escrow costs.

Thanking you in advance,

_____

Enclosure: ← Card

Request for Private Mortgage Insurance Information

UR

H O M E   R E A L T Y

_____ ← Date and address

_____
_____
_____

Dear _____:

Please send me information on your requirements for and costs of private mortgage insurance. Please also include several application packages.

I look forward to receiving the material and hope it will lead to a mutually beneficial relationship.

Yours truly,

_____

Enclosure: ← Card

Inquiry About Home Protection Warranty

UR
HOME REALTY

_____ ← Date and address

_____
_____
_____

Dear _____:

Please send me information, costs, and coverage for your home warranty programs, as well as several application packages.

I look forward to receiving the material and hope it will lead to a mutually beneficial relationship.

Yours truly,

_____

Enclosure: ← Card

Inquiry About Escrow Status for Closing

To:

CC: [J. Hirt and L. Scallon]

From: agent@urhome.com

Subject: Escrow Status [1 1 1 W. Jackson; Hirt, Scallon]

Dear _____:

Please provide me with the present status of the escrow for closing on [1 1 1 West Jackson Street], [Hirt, sellers, and Scallon, buyers].

If there is any problem that might prevent a [June 1] closing, please contact me at once. Thank you.

Yours truly,

_____

Order to Return or Turn Over Deposit

UR
HOME REALTY

_____ ← Date and address

_____
_____
_____

To: [1. Escrow agent 2. Attorney holding a deposit]

Dear _____:

You are holding an earnest money deposit for [$10,000], pursuant to a [purchase agreement] dated [October 1, 2012], in which [Joseph and Susan Scallon] agreed to buy [the home at 6116 Elm Street West] from [Ashley Dooley]. [Enclosed is a release authorization signed by (the Scallons and Mrs. Dooley).]

You are hereby authorized to [1. return 2. turn over] [1. the deposit 2. the sum of ($10,000)] to [1. Joseph and Susan Scallon 2. Ashley Dooley].

Yours truly,

_____

Enclosures: ← Card, copy of buyer/seller authorization to return or turn over
               deposit

cc: [Joseph and Susan Scallon, Ashley Dooley]

Note: This is an order to a third-party escrow holder about return of deposit money when the sale will not be completed. The sellers must agree to the return of the deposit to the buyers, or the buyers must agree to turn over their deposit to the seller.

CHAPTER

PERSONNEL LETTERS

Real Estate Career Night Announcement

Join Us for Real Estate Career Night

- Learn how many people have found new direction in their lives through real estate.

- Learn the following benefits that a professional career in real estate offers:

  - The personal satisfaction of helping others

  - The independence of planning your own work

  - Financial rewards directly related to your success in helping to meet housing needs

  - Constant mental stimulation in facing unique challenges

If you are a retiree, a homemaker reentering the workforce, a recent graduate, or someone simply interested in a career change, this is your opportunity to learn how a real estate career can meet your needs and to ask any questions you might have.

[Thursday, April 8]

[7:00 PM]

[Refreshments will be served.]

[UR Home Realty]

[473 N. Main]

[RSVP] [602-555-8200]

Note: This notice can be mailed on invitation stock as an invitation or mailed as a letter. It can also be used as a flyer. Good places to leave or post flyers are senior centers and over-55 senior housing developments.

New or Prospective Real Estate Salesperson Solicitation

UR
_____
H O M E   R E A L T Y

_____ ← Date and address

_____
_____
_____

Dear _____:

I understand you [1. are currently enrolled in a real estate license preparatory course   2. have applied to take your real estate salesperson's examination   3. have recently passed your real estate salesperson's examination]. I wish you success, and I hope you find a career in real estate that is as personally rewarding for you as it has been for many of us.

[UR Home Realty] is looking for people who are sincerely seeking a career, not just a job. People who want professional growth so they can meet the needs of others. People with integrity and motivation. These are the kinds of individuals who can be successful real estate salespersons.

If you feel your goals are compatible with ours, and you have not made a decision as to broker affiliation, call me so we can arrange to meet to discuss a possible career with [UR Home Realty]. We want you to learn about us as we learn about you.

Sincerely,

_____

Enclosure: ← Card

Note: Some states sell lists of names of applicants for licensing examinations, as well as lists of names of those who passed their examinations. Some license preparatory schools will also provide names of students.

Salesperson Solicitation—Retired

UR

HOME REALTY

_____ ← Date and address

_____
_____
_____

Dear _____:

Are you

Tired of Being Retired?

If you like people, have good character, and are not afraid to start a new career, I would like to meet with you.

I can offer you the personal satisfaction of helping others, a feeling of self-worth working in an independent environment, mental stimulation, and financial rewards earned by your success. After your license-training program, we will work with you and guide you in your career.

Interested? Then call [602-555-8200] today so we can meet to discuss a career in real estate.

Yours truly,

_____

Enclosure: ← Card

Note: This letter can be mailed to people living in over-55 retirement-oriented developments or modified for use as a flyer and distributed in retirement communities, as well as in senior centers.

Welcome New Agent (Large or Multioffice Broker)

UR

H O M E   R E A L T Y

_____ ← Date and address

_____
_____
_____

Dear _____:

Welcome to [UR Home Realty]!

Our goal at [UR Home Realty] is to serve the needs of buyers and sellers to the best of our abilities. To accomplish this goal, we must be knowledgeable professionals. Therefore, we encourage your professional growth, and we will do all we can to guide you in your success.

I look forward to a long and mutually beneficial association. If any problems arise or if we can provide any assistance, please let us know.

Sincerely,

_____

Enclosure: ← Card

Note: In all but the largest offices, the broker should meet persorally with the new salesperson.

Training Session Notice

To:

From: agent@urhome.com

Subject: Training Session

Attention All Sales Personnel!

Training Session:

[Wednesday, April 1, 9:00 AM to 10:00 AM (prior to caravan)]

Subject:

[Listing Techniques]

[If you are unable to attend, please contact (Jane Jones) as soon as possible.]

[Coffee and rolls will be served.]

Note: If the firm has multiple offices, include the location of the session.

Sales Meeting Notice

To:

From: agent@urhome.com

Subject: Sales Meeting

Attention All Sales Personnel!

Sales Meeting:

[Monday, June 17, 7:00 AM to 8:30 AM]

[Coffee and donuts will be served.]

[If you are unable to attend, please notify]

[John Jones]

[Extension 78]

[jjones@urhomerealty.net]

Note: If the firm has multiple offices, include the location of the meeting.

Notice to Salesperson of Missed Meeting

UR
H O M E   R E A L T Y

_____ ← Date and address

_____
_____
_____

Dear _____:

You were missed at the [training session on Wednesday, April 1, as well as the office meeting and property caravan on Wednesday, April 8]. If you have any difficulties, I would be happy to provide any advice or assistance that I can offer.

Our office works as a team, and we try to help each other. We also view training and office meetings as important functions to aid all personnel.

It is important that all team members share their knowledge, experience, and support. I look forward to your attendance and support in the future.

Sincerely,

_____

Note: Whenever possible, handle personnel matters in person rather than by letter. Do not demand that the salesperson attend meetings because such demands might be evidence that the salesperson is an employee rather than an independent contractor.

Notice to Salesperson—Unauthorized Absence

UR
H O M E   R E A L T Y

_____ ← Date and address

_____
_____
_____

Dear _____:

On [Wednesday, March 1], you were scheduled for [1. floor time 2. an open house at (111 Circle Drive)]. You were not present, and because I was not notified that you would be absent, no other arrangements were made.

When a salesperson misses [1. floor time, we have inadequate coverage, which results in wasted advertising dollars and lost opportunities 2. an open house, not only do we waste advertising dollars but also the potential is there to upset owners as well as buyers who have made a trip to see a home that is not open].

Although I realize there are legitimate emergencies, it is imperative that the office be notified as soon as possible of any absence when you are scheduled to be present.

Sincerely,

_____

Note: A personal meeting is the preferred way to handle a matter such as this.

Problem Notification

UR

H O M E   R E A L T Y

_____ ← Date and address

_____
_____
_____

Dear _____ :

I am sorry to say that I have received a complaint alleging [that you informed the buyer of 2101 Clement Avenue (Donald Riley) that the house was connected to city sewer when it was served by a septic system].

[1. Could you please meet with me   2. Could you please meet with our attorney and me] [on Friday, April 12, at 4:00 PM] [at 5 Crescent Boulevard, Suite 1800?]

[1. I have arranged a meeting with (Mr. Riley, you, and me) at (our office) at (4:00 PM on Thursday, April 12).   2. If you can come at (3:00 PM), it will give me a chance to get all the facts straight.]

Yours truly,

_____

Commission Dispute Between Agents

To:

From: agent@urhome

Subject: Commission [1 1 1 W. Jackson]

I would like to meet with you and [Charles Smith] in my office on [April 1], at [4:00 PM], to resolve the disagreement over the entitlement to the [1. listing 2. sales] commission for the [1. listing of 2. sale of] [1 1 1 West Jackson Street].

[Broker]

Office Dispute Decision

UR

H O M E   R E A L T Y

_____ ← Date and address

_____
_____
_____

Dear _____:

According to your [1. employment 2. independent contractor] agreement with [UR Home Realty], commission disputes within the office will be resolved by [binding broker arbitration].

On [April 11], I heard your claim for [one-half of the sales commission for the sale of the property at 111 West Jackson Street, as well as the claim of Emily Jones for the entire sales commission for the same sale].

Based on the information presented to me, [Emily Jones is entitled to the entire sales commission for the sale of 111 West Jackson Street].

Sincerely,

_____

Note: This letter can be used only if the salesperson's contract calls for binding arbitration by the broker. The preferred approach would be to notify the parties in person of your decision.

Salesperson Achievement—Congratulations

UR

H O M E   R E A L T Y

_____ ← Date and address

_____
_____
_____

Dear _____:

Congratulations on [1. your first sale over ($1,000,000) 2. your first exchange
3. exceeding your sales goal for (February) 4. being the top (1. selling 2. listing)
salesperson in our office for (February)]!

I hope this accomplishment is merely a prelude to even greater achievements. Use this
as just one stepping stone to the future.

Warmest regards,

_____

Special Recognition—Training Completion or Professional Designation

UR

H O M E   R E A L T Y

_____ ← Date and address

_____
_____
_____

Dear _____:

You may be justifiably proud of your accomplishments in [1. completing the Certified Residential Specialist (CRS) program   2. attaining the professional designation of Graduate of the REALTORS® Institute (GRI)]. I know that it wasn't easy, but I am sure the feeling of confidence, prestige within the industry, and most importantly, the ability to better serve buyers and sellers makes the time well spent.

Congratulations—not just from me, but from our entire profession!

Sincerely,

_____

[P.S. Enclosed is a copy of the press release that will inform our community of your accomplishment.]

Salesperson Award

UR
HOME REALTY

_____ ← Date and address

_____
_____
_____

Dear _____:

This is to inform you that you are the grand winner of [Salesperson of the Month for January]. This award was achieved with [your sales of $3,851,000].

You can claim the award of [a three-day Las Vegas holiday for two] at [Anderson Travel].

Our warmest congratulations,

_____

[P.S. Enclosed is a copy of the press release we issued about your accomplishment.]

Note: Awards should generally be made before the entire sales force. Notices, if used, should be by telegram, express courier service, or special delivery letter to emphasize the importance of the achievement.

Happy Birthday #1

UR
H O M E   R E A L T Y

_____ ← Date and address

_____
_____
_____

Dear _____:

Well, another year has passed. In retrospect, it has been a good year for you. Your fellow workers respect you as a knowledgeable and caring person. You are dedicated and have taken the reins of your own destiny. Most important, we regard you as our friend.

A very Happy Birthday, [Martin], from all of us.

_____   _____

_____   _____

_____   _____

Note: A letter is a warmer approach than just a card. A small gift such as a quality pen might be appropriate.

Happy Birthday #2

UR

H O M E   R E A L T Y

Happy Birthday, [Clarence]!

We all wish you the very best on your birthday:

Good Health

Good Friends

[Happy Family]

Prosperity

We hope you are with us at [UR Home Realty] to celebrate a great many more of them.
Again—a very Happy Birthday!

Note: The entire staff should sign. The card could be attached to a balloon anchored on the agent's desk with a box of candy or other small gift.

Wedding Anniversary

UR

H O M E   R E A L T Y

Dear _____:

My very best wishes to both of you on your wedding anniversary! As a small token of my personal regard for you, I have enclosed [a certificate for dinner for two at the Golden Palm].

It is my sincere hope that you have a joyful celebration of this and many more anniversaries.

Very sincerely,

_____

Note: Include the names of both husband and wife in the salutation.

Anniversary with Firm

UR
HOME REALTY

_____ ← Date and address

_____
_____
_____

Dear _____:

I don't know if you noticed, but it's our anniversary. On [June 1], it will have been [five] years since you joined [UR Home Realty]. These years have been filled with many successes and a lot of hard work. During this time, you have helped to make possible the dream of home ownership for many families.

I want you to realize that your efforts have not gone unnoticed or unappreciated. I am proud to have you with the firm and look forward to a great many more anniversaries.

Congratulations!

_____

Birth of Son or Daughter

UR
HOME REALTY

Dear [Joan and Bob]:

My warmest congratulations on the birth of your [1. daughter 2. son]! Little [1. Mary Elizabeth 2. John Martin] has a [1. father 2. mother] [1. she 2. he] can be proud of.

This small gift is a token of my regard for you and the joy I share with you on this miraculous event.

Very sincerely,

_____

Death in Agent's Family

UR
HOME REALTY

Dear _____:

Please accept my sincere condolences to you [and your son] on your recent loss. I know how much you thought of [Mary Jane] and can understand your feelings at this time.

[Mary Jane] brought joy to the lives of [her] family and friends, and [her] memory will live on in those whose lives [she] influenced.

[According to your wishes, I have made a donation to (The American Cancer Society) in (Mary Jane's) name.]

Thinking of you,

_____

Note: This personal note is sent in addition to any flowers you might send for the funeral. A handwritten note is more personal than a typed message.

Death of Salesperson or Associate

UR
HOME REALTY

Dear _____:

I wish to offer my personal condolences to you. [Mary] *was* [1. an associate broker   2. a salesperson] *with* [UR Home Realty] *for* [1. (seven) years   2. all too short a time]. [She] *was liked and respected by all of us as well as by the many clients whose real estate needs* [she] *helped to meet.* [Mary] *gave unsparingly of* [herself] *in helping others.*

I share in your feeling of loss and want you to know that [Mary] *will be truly missed.*

[According to your wishes], *I have made a donation to* [1. the American Cancer Society   2. the Multiple Sclerosis Society] *in* [Mary's] *name.*

Yours truly,

_____

Note: This letter would be sent to a spouse, life partner, or parent upon the death of an agent. A handwritten note is more personal than a typed message.

Agent Who Voluntarily Left Office

UR
HOME REALTY

_____ ← Date and address

_____
_____
_____

Dear _____:

I would like to take this opportunity to thank you for your professional efforts with [UR Home Realty] over the past [five years].

I wish you [1. happiness 2. success] for your future. [I want you to know that you will always have a home with (UR Home Realty).]

[Of course, you will promptly receive all commissions upon closing of transactions, in accord with our agreement.]

[We would appreciate the return of (office keys, signs, and so on) to us as soon as practical.]

[If in the future you need a recommendation, do not hesitate to contact me.]

Sincerely,

_____

Enclosure: ← Card

Note: This letter will help to keep your relationship open with an employee who may have left for perceived "greener pastures." It will also aid in future agent cooperation if the agent joins a competing firm.

Letter of Recommendation

UR

H O M E   R E A L T Y

_____ ← Date and address

_____

_____

_____

[1. Dear _____: 2. To Whom It May Concern:]

[Janet Jones] worked for [UR Home Realty] from [August 1998] to [June 2005] as a [1. real estate sales associate   2. REALTOR-Associate®]. [Janet] always exhibited the utmost integrity and a sincere desire to help others in meeting their housing needs. [I would hire (Janet Jones) again without hesitation.]

Yours truly,

_____

Notice to Salesperson—Termination

UR
HOME REALTY

_____ ← Date and address

_____
_____
_____

Dear _____ :

I am very sorry to inform you that we are unable to retain your services as a [1. sales associate 2. REALTOR-Associate®] with [UR Home Realty]. [1. I have enclosed your real estate license. 2. Our office will strictly honor your contract rights for sales and listings in progress. 3. Please drop off your office keys and return all (signs and lockboxes) as soon as possible.]

I wish you every success in your future endeavors, and if I can be of any help to you or if you have any questions, please contact me personally.

Sincerely,

_____

Note: Normally, you should handle this in a face-to-face meeting. Avoid criticism or any accusations of dishonesty, because either could later be construed as libel. This letter should be sent by registered mail.

C H A P T E R

13

PRESS RELEASES

Transmittal Letter—Press Release

UR
HOME REALTY

_____ ← Date and address

_____
_____
_____

Dear _____:

Enclosed is a press release [as well as a photograph with caption] concerning [Frederick Schmidt, who has recently been awarded the Certified Residential Specialist designation].

[We believe this significant achievement deserves community recognition.]

If you have any questions or desire further information, please contact me.

Yours truly,

_____

Enclosures: ← Card, photo, and press release

Note: Use masking tape as a hinge on the back of the photo so that the caption can be read below the 5-by-7 high-contrast, black-and-white glossy. Be certain to identify persons shown, from left to right in each row, beginning with the front row.

Some newspapers prefer to receive press releases by e-mail with high resolution digital photo attachments. Check with your local newspapers as to their preferences.

Important Buyer

[Retired Banker Chooses Meadowbrook]

Mr. and Mrs. [Angus McCook] have recently purchased [a new home on Clancy Lane in Meadowbrook]. [Mr. McCook was active in banking for 40 years, starting as a teller with the Midvale Bank and rising to the presidency of the Newport Banking Group, one of the largest bank holding companies in the state.]

[The McCooks] indicated that they were attracted to [Meadowbrook] because of [1. the choice of several outstanding golf courses 2. its general country atmosphere 3. its proximity to the amenities of urban life]. The purchase was arranged through the [Meadowbrook office of UR Home Realty].

Enclosure: ← Photo

Note: A press release about a buyer is appropriate when the buyer has a distinguished or interesting background. Photos with captions should be included. Consider a photo of the buyer(s) in front of the property showing a sold sign. Always obtain the buyer's permission before publicizing a purchase.

Important Sale

[Smith Building Sold]

[Jim Anderson] of [UR Home Realty] recently sold [the Smith Building] at [5 Commercial Avenue]. The former owners, [Alice and Gertrude Smith], owned this landmark property for [45] years.

The purchasers, [Thomas and Anna Blake] of [San Juno], have indicated that they will [1. extensively remodel the property   2. move their offices to the property]. [Mr. Blake is president of Blake Motors in Covina.]

[This sale brings the first quarter sales of (UR Home Realty) to over ($27 million), which is an increase of (16) percent over last year's sales. (Joseph Lane, vice president of sales,) has indicated that interest in large commercial properties such as the Smith Building has increased significantly and he predicts continued sales increases in the foreseeable future.]

Enclosure: ⟵ Photo

Note: If a building is well known or has historical significance, a press release would be appropriate when it is listed for sale or sold. Include a captioned photo of the property, possibly with the buyers and the agent in front of the property. Always obtain permission of both buyer and seller to publicize a sale.

Important Sale Listing

[Carson Building] To Be Sold

[Jim Anderson] of [UR Home Realty] announced that UR Home Realty has been selected by [the Newport Development Corporation] to be its agent for the sale of [the historic Carson Building] at [139 West Main Street in Hortonville]. The [12-story building is home to 14 law firms].

The [Newport Development Corporation] has indicated that the property is being sold [to consolidate its investments in the San Bruno area].

Enclosure: ⟵ Photo

Note: See the note with the previous press release.

Groundbreaking

Groundbreaking—[Woodlake Village]

[Wilson Developers] held an official groundbreaking for the new [122 single-family-home Woodlake Village development] on [Wednesday, March 1].

Located [on the northwest corner of Dunn Road and Woodlake Parkway], the [three- and four-bedroom family homes] will feature [1. up to (2,400) square feet 2. three-car garages, tile roofs, and Eurostyle kitchens].

[Peggy Johnson,] project sales coordinator for [UR Home Realty] and the exclusive sales agent for [Woodlake Village], has indicated that the choice location, coupled with moderate prices, starting at [$295,500] with [5 percent] financing, has already created an exceptional word-of-mouth interest in the development. According to [Johnson], the early reservations have been primarily from [1. professionals in the real estate and construction industries 2. telecom professionals].

Enclosure: ← Photo

Note: For groundbreaking ceremonies, consider including a captioned photograph with local civic leaders and a builder representative, as well as an agent of your firm, wearing hard hats. An artist's rendering of a model home would also be appropriate.

Subdivision Opening

Grand Opening—[Woodlake Village]

The grand opening of [Wilson Development's] new [Woodlake Village] is scheduled for [Saturday and Sunday, June 5 and 6]. Located [on the northwest corner of Dunn Road and Woodlake Parkway], the development features [three- and four-bedroom family homes starting at $329,000, with 5½ percent financing available]. All homes include [three-car garages, tile roofs, and Eurostyle kitchens].

[Peggy Johnson,] the [sales coordinator] for [UR Home Realty], which is the exclusive sales agent for the project, has indicated that exceptional interest has developed in [Woodlake Village] due to [its choice location and the moderate pricing policy].

According to [Johnson], the grand opening will feature [six decorator-furnished models, and there will be refreshments and gifts for opening-day visitors].

Enclosure: ⟵ Photo

Note: You should include a photo or artist's rendering of one of the models. Placing ads on the opening generally ensures publication of your press release.

First Sale in Subdivision

First Sale Made at [English Village]

[UR Home Realty], the exclusive sales agent for [English Village], has announced that [Dr. and Mrs. Timothy Marks] are the first home purchasers in [the exclusive enclave of 16 estate homes in Bellwood]. [A pediatrician, Dr. Marks is on the staff of Mercy Hospital.]

The [Marks] chose a [3,600 square-foot English country design]. According to [Mrs. Marks], the couple decided on [English Village] because of [its huge lots, scenic views, quality design and construction, as well as the country ambience, which is so important with four small children].

[Currently, three of the estate homes are under construction, with the Marks's home scheduled for completion by August 15.]

Enclosure: ⟵ Photo

Note: For a press release that provides information about a buyer, be certain to obtain permission from the buyer. A captioned picture of the purchasing family standing in front of the home, even if the home is not completed, would be appropriate. In addition to publicity about your firm, a press release such as this one significantly reduces the possibility that the buyer will attempt to avoid the purchase closing.

Milestone Sale in Subdivision

[(100th) Sale Announced for Orchard Heights]

[Henry Ammenson], [project director] for [UR Home Realty], has announced that the [100th new home since November in Orchard Heights has been sold]. According to [Ammenson], this subdivision has been one of the most successful in the area because of the tremendous value offered in housing at a premier location. The problem has been not being able to build the homes fast enough. [Ammenson indicates that, at the present sales rate, the entire subdivision will be sold out by June 1.]

Enclosure: ⟵ Photo

Note: Consider a captioned photograph of the buying family in front of their new home. Never distribute a press release about a transaction, a buyer, or a seller without written permission from the people involved.

$5 Million in Sales in 5 Weeks

[UR Home Realty Salesperson Sets Sales Record]

[Jennifer Wu of UR Home Realty] has closed [$5 million] in sales in [5 weeks]. [Jennifer] has been a sales associate with [UR Home Realty] for [3 years] after spending [9 years as a computer programmer]. [Jennifer and her husband] live[s] in [Newhall] with [their] [3 children].

Enclosure: ← Photo

Office Opening or Relocation

[1. UR Home Realty Opens Newhall Office   2. UR Home Realty Expands]

[UR Home Realty] has announced [1. the opening of a (second) office (in the Murray Building at 136 West 31st Street in Lynnwood) 2. the relocation of its (Lynnwood) office to the (Murray Building at 136 West 31st Street).]

According to [Thomas Johnson, president of UR Home Realty], the [1. expansion 2. move] was necessary to better meet the needs of [Lynnwood] residents.

Although the office will specialize in [residential sales], its services will also include [investment sales and property management]. [The new office will also coordinate the sales of several new subdivisions in the area.] [UR Home Realty] currently has [more than 60 salespeople with total sales last year exceeding $500 million, making this firm one of the fastest-growing brokerage offices in the county]!

Enclosure: ← Photo

Note: Consider a captioned photograph of the entire office staff in front of the new office or with a For Sale sign having a Sold banner.

New Associate or Salesperson

[Henry Gibbs] Joins [UR Home Realty]

[Thomas Flynn], [general manager] of [UR Home Realty], announced that [Henry Gibbs] recently joined the firm as [1. a sales associate 2. a REALTOR-Associate® 3. an associate broker]. [Gibbs] will be involved with [home sales, primarily in the West Valley].

[Gibbs] is [a graduate of Syracuse University and has spent 12 years as a food broker in Chicago]. [He] obtained [his] real estate license [two years ago, and he was previously associated with Boniface Construction Company, selling new homes in the Bellwood Heights development]. [Gibbs is a member of Thunderbird Country Club and resides in Bellwood Heights with his wife, Eileen, and their two daughters.]

Enclosure: ⟵ Photo

Note: Send a captioned photo with all personnel press releases.

Promotion or Appointment

New [Sales Manager] [UR Home Realty]

[Henry Clyde, president of UR Home Realty,] has announced that [Jane Jones] has been appointed [sales manager] of [UR Home Realty]. [Jones] brings a wealth of experience to the position. [She] was formerly associated with [Smith Realty] as [assistant sales manager]. [Jones has had over (eight)] years of experience in [1. sales 2. real estate sales]. [Jones] has been with [UR Home Realty] for [four years]. [Jones has received numerous honors, including membership in the prestigious UR Home Realty Ten Million Dollar Roundtable.]

[1. Jones received her bachelor's degree in business from Yale University. 2. Jones attended New York University.] [She] lives with [her] family in [Midvale Heights]. [She has two children, John, nine years old, and Tammy, six.] [Her husband, Tony, teaches English at South High School.] [Jones] is active [in Soroptimists and as an assistant Girl Scout leader].

Enclosure: ⟵ Photo

Note: Consider a captioned photo of a broker with the new [sales manager] either in front of the office or near an office sign. If the person did not graduate from a school, you can use "attended." If the person graduated, indicate "graduated from" or the degree received.

Professional Designation

[Chris Jones Earns Professional Designation]

[Chris Jones], a[n] [1. sales associate 2. associate broker 3. REALTOR-Associate®]
with [UR Home Realty], has recently earned the coveted [Certified Residential
Specialist (CRS)] designation. This [is the highest] professional award of the [Residential Sales Council] and is awarded only after a [1. REALTOR® 2. real estate professional] has met [high standards for experience and has also completed a rigorous
course of training]. [Jones] is now one of just a few real estate professionals in [our
community] who may use [CRS] after [his] name.

[Jones has been a real estate professional for 17 years. He is a graduate of Notre
Dame, where he earned his degree in marketing and is a Gulf War veteran. He lives in
Westwood with his wife, Ellen, and their two daughters. Jones is active in the Rotary
Club and is a deacon at Westwood Community Church.]

Enclosure: ⟵ Photo

Note: The fact that a press release deals with a salesperson who is a Gulf War Veteran
helps create a positive image of that salesperson and should be mentioned.

Sales Award

Salesperson of the [1. Month 2. Year]

[Joseph Evans], [sales manager] of [UR Home Realty], has announced that [Patricia
Jones] has been named [sales associate] of the [1. month 2. year].

During [1. March 2. the past year], [Jones] has [1. sold 2. listed] [1. more than $6
million in real estate 2. 19 properties]. [Jones] has been associated with [UR Home
Realty] [1. since 1998 2. for seven years]. Before joining [UR Home Realty], [she]
was [a professor of zoology at Western State University]. [Jones lives in Middletown
with her husband and four children.]

Enclosure: ⟵ Photo

Note: Enclose a photo of a broker presenting the salesperson with the award.

Sale of Real Estate Firm

New Owner Announced for [UR Home Realty]

[UR Home Realty] has announced that the firm has been sold [by its founder, Angus Johnson, to the firm's general manager, Thomas Flynn. Johnson founded UR Home Realty in 1947, and it has been the oldest real estate firm in the county under the same ownership.]

[UR Home Realty] currently has [62 salespeople operating from their offices at 922 West Broadway]. [Johnson] estimates that since its founding, the firm has sold over [25,000] properties, with total sales [in the hundreds of millions of dollars].

[Flynn has been associated with UR Home Realty for 11 years, starting as a salesperson, and has served the last four years as general manager. Flynn, who is a business graduate of Michigan State University, indicates that the firm's name, as well as the philosophy and policies of Johnson, will continue.]

Enclosure: ⟵ Photo

Note: Include a photograph showing both the former owner (if possible) and the successor.

CHAPTER 14

MISCELLANEOUS LETTERS

Letter to Newspaper About Ad Copy—Transmittal

UR
HOME REALTY

_____ ← Date and address

_____
_____
_____

Dear _____ :

I wish to run the following ads [1. from (Sunday, April 3,) through (Saturday, April 9,) 2. on (Sunday, April 3,)] in the classified section under the following categories:

Category: _____
_____
_____
_____

Category: _____
_____
_____
_____

Please bill these ads to our account.

Yours truly,

_____

Enclosure: ← Card

Note: Give any instructions about size or style of type, if applicable.

Notice to Newspaper of Mistake in Advertisement

UR
H O M E   R E A L T Y

_____ ← Date and address

_____
_____
_____

Attention: Classified Advertisement Department Editor

[1. Dear editor: 2. To whom it may concern:]

On [September 10], we placed an ad under the category [Real Estate] to run on [Sunday, September 16].

The ad was to read as follows: _____
_____
_____

Due to your error, the ad appeared on [September 17] on page [37], [under the category (Appliances)], [and read as follows]: _____
_____
_____

Because of the error, [1. the effectiveness of the ad was materially diminished 2. the ad was of no benefit to our firm]. We therefore expect [1. an appropriate adjustment because of your error 2. the ad charge to be fully credited on our next billing 3. the ad to be run on (October 12) without charge].

Yours truly,

_____

Enclosures: ← Card, ad copy

Note: You may wish to use a yellow highlighter to indicate an error in the ad copy or placement.

Charity Ticket Response

UR

H O M E   R E A L T Y

_____ ← Date and address

_____
_____
_____

Dear _____:

Enclosed is our check for [$30] for [two] tickets. The remaining tickets are enclosed.

We are always happy to provide assistance to local organizations. We wish you good luck on your event.

Yours truly,

_____

Enclosures: ← Card, check, tickets

Note: Charities generally send out books of tickets. This response allows you to be positive without purchasing all the tickets.

Christmas Card Caption

May the joyous holiday spirit

extend throughout the coming year.

Wishing you and yours a very special

Season's Greetings

from all of us at

[UR Home Realty]!

Note: This short season's greetings would be appropriate with a photograph of your staff and families and/or with the personal signatures of your staff.

INDEX OF LETTERS

Notes